Critical issues in New Zealand society

Gender, Culture, and Power

Critical issues in New Zealand society

General editors: Steve Maharey and Paul Spoonley

Gender, Culture, and Power
Challenging New Zealand's Gendered Culture

Bev James
Kay Saville-Smith

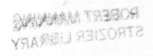
Auckland
Oxford University Press
Melbourne Oxford New York

Oxford University Press

Oxford University Press, Walton Street, Oxford OX2 6DP

OXFORD NEW YORK TORONTO
DELHI BOMBAY CALCUTTA MADRAS KARACHI
PETALING JAYA SINGAPORE HONG KONG TOKYO
NAIROBI DAR ES SALAAM CAPE TOWN
MELBOURNE AUCKLAND
and associated companies in
BERLIN IBADAN

Oxford is a trade mark of Oxford University Press

First published 1989
Bev James and Kay Saville-Smith 1989

ISBN 0 19 558201 2

Designed by Hilary Ravenscroft
Photoset in Bembo by Typeset Graphics
and printed in Hong Kong
Published by Oxford University Press
1A Matai Road, Greenlane, Auckland 3, New Zealand

Contents

Editors' Preface

Our concern as editors of this Critical Issues series has been to encourage particular social scientists, who have something distinctive to say about an aspect of New Zealand society, to state their argument in a clear, concise, and readable fashion. While providing an introduction to the debate as a whole, authors have been asked to take a position and argue it through, suggesting what might be done to resolve a particular set of problems. It is our belief that while all points of view deserve a hearing, there is a need today to have people with strong beliefs to state their case so that a real debate can emerge.

The first book in the Critical Issues series was *Racism and Ethnicity*. In this, the second book, Bev James and Kay Saville-Smith argue that New Zealand is a gendered society. The authors suggest that the notions of masculinity and femininty which have developed from the nineteenth century, when a gendered culture was established, along with the exchanges between masculine and feminine worlds, are critical to an understanding of power and inequality in New Zealand. They go on to argue that a gendered culture has become a major social problem in contemporary New Zealand. In matters such as alcohol consumption and sport, or driving, the gendered culture has produced values and behaviours which are very destructive. The costs are borne by both men and women. The argument presented here is an unequivocable and challenging one, and fulfils the purpose of the series admirably.

Steve Maharey and Paul Spoonley
Series Editors

Acknowledgements

This project has been made possible through the efforts and goodwill of many. Most immediately for their work in helping to transform drafts into the finished product, we would like to acknowledge the support of series editors, Steve Maharey and Paul Spoonley and thank particularly Anne French and Harriet Bennett Allan of Oxford University Press, for their help in transforming drafts into the finished product and for their general encouragement. Donna Cook was always efficient and good humoured in typing up the manuscript.

Less direct, but nevertheless formative influences on our ideas presented here should also be recognized. Kay owes much to Geoff Fougere, Peggy Koopman-Boyden, Rosemary Novitz, Chris Wilkes, and Bill Wilmott, all of whom have contributed greatly to her development as a sociologist. It is hoped they are not disappointed with the result. Bev owes a debt to those involved in her Kawerau research. It was in this practical fieldwork context that she began to make connections between the inequalities of sex, race, and class.

Many have encouraged us in writing this book. The comments of those who attended our paper on this subject at the 1987 Sociological Association of Australia and New Zealand Conference in Sydney made us feel the project was worthwhile. Bob Connell was particularly encouraging and we appreciated his insightful comments. Rosemary Novitz was one of the first to listen to our, at that time, rather garbled intentions, and Norma Te Purei has always shown ready interest and given us feedback. We thank them both. We would also like to thank Murray Ball for his creative insights into New Zealand's gendered culture. His cartoons made the task of writing this book lots of fun.

Finally, we would like to thank each other for listening, being patient, and successfully putting the ideal of co-operative work into practise. In hope of the future, we would like to dedicate this book to Nina and James.

Introduction

For those committed to social justice, living in New Zealand is a frustrating experience. We live in a society where inequalities between those who do and do not own productive property, between men and women, and between Pākehā and Polynesian (especially between Pākehā and Māori) are well documented. Yet old ideas that New Zealand is an egalitarian society linger, while many of those who do acknowledge that some groups are persistently excluded from many of the resources in our society accept such inequalities as necessary, inevitable, and, thus, ultimately acceptable.

This is not to suggest that New Zealanders are unconcerned about the plight of disadvantaged individuals or those who fall victim to ill health or violence. We expend time, energy, and money trying to 'put our world to rights' by pursuing law and order campaigns, lobbying to ban gangs, pornography, and cruelty to animals, worrying about the road toll, and supporting charities ranging from the hugely successful telethons to the Salvation Army and Corso. We spend many unrecorded and unpaid hours sitting on worthy committees and working for service clubs. Whenever a natural disaster strikes, even the poorest regions mobilize their frequently meagre resources to send food and clothing to disaster victims. We are, as individuals, not without compassion. However, there is a vast disjuncture between the compassion we show as individuals and the structural organization of our society.

This society is structured around unequal access to resources and rewards. From those structures arises a sort of collective callousness which allows us to leave many homeless, unemployed, lacking in health care, and with few opportunities to enjoy the good things this society has to offer. At times, callousness becomes sheer brutality. We live in a society in which domestic violence, alcohol abuse, and road-killings are, if not actually accepted, at least commonplace.

For those actively concerned with such problems as public and domestic violence, alcohol abuse, and the 'accidental' deaths which occur weekly on our roads, the campaigns must seem unending and depressingly ineffective. Activists seeking a fairer society often feel similarly. The disjuncture between the compassion of individuals and collective insensibility makes progressive social change in New Zealand seem almost unattainable.

There are a number of fundamental problems facing those who wish
to achieve a fairer society in New Zealand. Among the most significant
is the need to relate the popular and real concerns of individuals
regarding order, violence, and powerlessness to a critical analysis of the
way in which our society is structured. It is essential that we explore
the way certain organizational procedures, which systematically, though
often unintentionally, privilege one group over another, are able to
endure. Exposing the connections between 'private troubles and public
issues' (Mills, 1970: chapter 1) is central not only to understanding how
a society works, but also to the pursuit of social justice.

The second fundamental problem for activists is how to make effective
political alliances when the lines of inequality are complex and cross-
cutting. Can the Pākehā poor ally with Māori (some of whom may be
poor and some of whom may not be, but who are all victims of racism),
when often racism is perpetrated by the Pākehā poor themselves? What
hopes are there for alliances between working men and women seeking
sexual equality with men, when working-class men have traditionally
used wives' economic dependency as a tool in wage bargaining with
employers? The resolution of this problem cannot be solved with mere
goodwill, nor by glossing over real differences in interests between the
under-resourced (the unpropertied, women, and Māori) in our society.
Nor can it be resolved by asserting, a priori, the primacy of one set of
inequalities relative to the others.

Traditional ways in which radical social theorists and activists have
explained social inequalities tend to give priority to one form of
inequality or oppressive relationship over other forms. Thus, one of these
(sex, class, or race) is presented as more basic, more important, and,
consequently, as taking political priority or precedence in the struggle
for a fair society. Along these lines, the radical feminist Firestone (1972)
argues that all inequalities stem from men's oppression of women. Thus,
with regard to inequalities between ethnic groups, she states that racism
can only be understood in terms of power relations in the family: '...
the races are no more than the various parents and siblings in the Family
of Man' (Firestone, 1972: 105). Racism, like all inequalities, is thus
reduced to the antagonism between the sexes. By defining the family
in stark biological terms as the institution in which women are
subordinated and exploited because of their reproductive physiology,
Firestone (1972: 17) asserts that not only are sex conflict and inequality
based on the physiological differences between women and men, but
so too are inequalities such as class and race.

In terms of practical, political activity, this type of argument places
the oppression of women in a privileged role, to be tackled first. While
some women (and, perhaps, some men) may feel this is consistent with

their personal experience, others may find this an inadequate and inappropriate strategy, given their particular class and race. This type of argument is also inadequate because it fails to develop a theory of the role of historical, social, and cultural conditions in the formation of social structures. Instead, it reduces complex social phenomena to simple biological factors. This has profound implications for those concerned with the problem of social change. As Barrett (1980: 13) observes, biological determinist explanations are inevitably reactionary, for 'if particular social arrangements are held to be "naturally" given, there is little we can do to change them'.

An alternative way of dealing with the problem of different oppressions is to explain them as derivatives of the mechanisms of a class society. This explanation is found in Bedggood's (1980) Marxist analysis of New Zealand's social structure. Bedggood (1980: 87–8) argues that women are exploited by the capitalist labour process, which both relies on women's domestic labour to reproduce the labour power of workers and pays women workers lower wages than men as a means of controlling the overall level of wages. Bedggood (1980: 92) sums up the relation of women's oppression to the class system by saying that it is '. . . historically a *means to the end* of class exploitation; that is, the expropriation of surplus labour of one class by another'. Thus, women's domestic and paid labour are instrumental in the reproduction of the working class for the benefit of capital.

Male members of the working class are depicted as merely the agents of the capitalist class's oppression of women who, in return, gain certain privileges, notably more secure and higher paid jobs (Bedggood, 1980: 92). This explanation suggests that women's oppression will be overcome once there is a socialist revolution. The interests of women are assumed to be the same as the interests of the working class, for whom a revolution in the mode of production is necessary for liberation. The status of women in socialist societies, such as Eastern Europe (Scott, 1976) and China (Wolfe, 1985), shows that while socialism may go some way towards providing women with equality, it is by no means sufficient. Most importantly, the Marxist explanation of women's oppression leaves unexplored the benefits that working-class men gain from their control over and exploitation of women as unpaid workers in the home and community. The Marxist position also ignores other important aspects of women's oppression, such as domestic violence and rape. Clearly, women's ability to obtain resources and status in society is determined by more than the capitalist relations of production. It is also determined by the legitimate authority of men to exert control over women, particularly through the institution of the family. Classical Marxist analyses, such as Bedggood's, fail to explain this.

With regard to inequalities deriving from race, Bedggood attributes these to the ways in which capitalist productive relations are conducted. Specifically, he argues that racial minorities have been used by European colonizers as a 'reserve army of labour' to fill the changing labour requirements of capitalist production. For example:

The Maori migration from rural to urban areas with the expansion of domestic manufacturing performed the role of the floating reserve army, filling the most low-skilled and low-paid jobs so long as the demand for workers grew. . . when the expansion began to slow, and when the restructuring of the economy accelerates the process of labour-shedding, it is mainly the Polynesian. . . reserve army which is thrown out of work. (Bedggood, 1980: 85.)

As with the problem of women's oppression, the problem of racial oppression cannot be reduced to economic requirements. Racism has a history of its own that includes more than just economic exploitation. Furthermore, as with the case of women, the interests of (in New Zealand) the Polynesian working class and the Pākehā working class are simply not synonymous. A good example of this is the issue of Māori land. Māori interests in regaining control over their lands are often opposed by Pākehā working-class people who regard this as privileged access to resources.

Inequalities of class and race cannot be explained by referring to the structures of conflict between the sexes, as Firestone attempts to do. Equally, Bedggood's attempt to explain women's oppression and racism by referring to the antagonism between the capitalist and the working class is inadequate. Awatere's expression of Māori sovereignty attempts to overcome these difficulties and the exclusion of a Māori voice in these analyses, by asserting that hierarchies of race, class, and sex are separate, though with significant connections between them. However, she tends to subsume inequalities of class and sex to racism. For example, Awatere (1984: 14) conceptualizes white culture as inherently racist because New Zealand was founded on the basis of racial conflict, stemming from the assumed racial interests of a colonizing power. In turn, this racial conflict led to the economic oppression of the Māori (Awatere 1984: 15), and the specific oppression of Māori women (Awatere 1984: 27). The political solution is seen to be Māori sovereignty.

The notion of white culture as a racist culture, which is inherent to Awatere's discussion, limits the analysis of inequality. By prioritizing racism over other forms of oppression, a historically specific form of capitalism (colonization) is conflated with the racist features of an alleged international white culture (Awatere 1984: 60-4). Colonization thus becomes primarily a racist activity, and the processes of capitalism are obscured. Furthermore, such an analysis makes it difficult to explore other aspects of Māori experiences, for example, the involvement of some Māori in bourgeois activities and the power of Māori men over Māori women. Ultimately these analyses all identify one system of oppression as determining all others. We consider that prioritizing inequality in this way is inappropriate. No one heirarchy can be demonstrated to be primary. Indeed the whole debate is futile and rests on an inadequate conceptualization of social life.

Brittan and Maynard (1984: 2) argue that when we use reductionist biological, cultural, or economic explanations of oppression, we risk 'missing critical dimensions of personal and social experience'. In particular, they accuse those taking up these primacy positions of ignoring the subjective definitions that the oppressed give to their experiences and neglecting the intentional nature of human actions. At many points, our criticisms of the primacy debate converge with Brittan and Maynard's concerns. With them we would argue that the hierarchies of sex, class, and race are not, as the primacy debate implies, pre-given and timeless categories. They are, instead, outcomes of historical and material processes through which social existence is created and perpetuated. We agree with Brittan and Maynard also that people's experiences of what it is to be a member of a particular sex or class, or to be defined in terms of race, is determined by their particular place in time and space. On the other hand, we diverge from the ideas Brittan and Maynard present to deal with the problem of primacy. Brittan and Maynard (1984: 5) appear to suggest that oppressive systems neither require an institutional base, nor any direct connection with structural processes. For them, the most crucial unit of analysis is the arena of individuals' immediate interaction, one with another. According to Brittan and Maynard (1984: 7), the:

terms of oppression . . . are also shaped . . . by the way in which oppressors and oppressed continuously have to renegotiate, reconstruct and re-establish their relative positions in respect to benefits and power. In the final analysis 'oppression is where you find it', and this is almost everywhere.

This position is unsatisfactory. Instead of challenging the traditional conceptual dichotomies between macro and micro worlds, structure and agency, society and individual, public and private, they reinforce these. This is achieved by an implicit denial that individuals institutionalize the routines of everyday life. Brittan and Maynard neglect structure as much as many of those they criticize neglect agency. Far from there being a separation between what Brittan and Maynard (1984: 7,4) refer to as 'history, culture, and the sexual and social division of labour' and the 'minutiae of everyday life', they are indivisible.

According to our perceptions, inequalities of sex, class, and race are not related just because each hierarchy is socially constructed through subjective, individual interactions between oppressor and oppressed. Rather, inequalities of race, class, and sex emerge out of the very material conditions of people's lives. They arise out of the organization of production and reproduction.

In essence, we cannot accept the primacy debate. To argue that one hierarchy, whether it be race, sex, or class, is a generalized determinant of all social existence inflates what are in reality specific, concrete experiences. At the same time, we cannot accept the subjectivist position of Brittan and Maynard because this tends to divorce personal experience from the institutional structure of society. Both schema, for different reasons, risk recasting what are social and political issues concerning inequality into moral issues. Too easily, attempts to identify the connections between different oppressions degenerate into a competition to establish who is 'most oppressed'. Oppression becomes a moral dilemma for those defined as oppressors, and the 'true' assessment of oppression is seen as the prerogative of those who claim to be oppressed. Under these circumstances, dissension and condemnation among those seeking a more just society is almost inevitable.

Our project is to provide a general analysis of New Zealand society to facilitate the pursuit of a fairer society. We do not suggest specific tactics for activists. These must be created in relation to the specific circumstances with which individuals and groups are confronted at any particular moment and with regard to the interests and constraints of those involved. Rather, we aim to provide a new view of New Zealand which connects the popular concerns of our time (the maintenance of order, domestic and public violence, and alcohol abuse) with the structural arrangement of our society.

We, like many others, see sex, race, and class as the major lines of exclusion and exploitation in this society. The problem for us all is how do they relate together? Why do they persist? In this book, we explore the notion that New Zealand is a 'gendered culture', a culture in which the structures of masculinity and femininity are central to the formation of society as a whole. Our analysis of the gendered culture involves certain assumptions about sex inequalities and the relationship between these and other structures of inequality, notably race and class. Specifically, we argue that the oppression of women should *not* be seen as the most fundamental dynamic of our society. To speak of New Zealand as a gendered culture does not imply that sex inequalities are more important than other inequalities nor that political action should be solely concentrated on the struggle between the sexes. Rather, it is argued that the gendered culture should be challenged because it enables hierarchies of sex, race, and class to be maintained.

What is it Really Between Cheeky Hobson and the Dog?

One of New Zealand's most successful films has been Murray Ball's *The Dog's Tail Tale*. Its international release drew, apart from the predictable jingoism which accompanies many of New Zealand's international actions, a degree of ambivalence. Would the overseas viewer recognize that the New Zealand portrayed was a fiction? Would they understand something as inexorably indigenous as *The Dog's Tail Tale?*

The Dog's Tail Tale may be fiction, but it represents and explores the major preoccupation of our culture: the assumption of masculinity and femininity, the integration of individuals into a gendered culture. The *Footrot Flats* strips, and to some extent the film, can be read as a commentary on gender relations: what it means to be women and men; how women and men relate. The struggle is one between 'mateship' and mating. This is the rift which dominates New Zealand's cultural expressions.

Despite the reality of inequalities of race, sex, and class, not one of these constitutes the predominant motif of New Zealand society. The visitor does not leave with a memory of a culture of poverty contrasting with a culture of wealth. In comparison with the public symbols of wealth and inequality embodied in the stately homes and aristocracy of Great Britain and Europe, the inner city ghettos and decay of North America, or the vast glittering shopping complexes which nudge squatter shacks in Asia, the deep structural inequalities associated with race, sex, and class in New Zealand are virtually hidden.

One is not confronted with inequality so much as difference, particularly that difference which New Zealanders like to see as most natural, the differences between men and women. The division is between masculine and feminine worlds. New Zealand is a society in which men are keen and women are definitely not blokes.

New Zealand is, what we term, a *gendered culture.* That is, a culture in which the intimate and structural expressions of social life are divided according to gender. Notions of masculinity and femininity are a pervasive metaphor which shape not merely relations between the sexes, but are integral to the systematic maintenance of other structures of inequality as well. Inequalities of sex, race, and class in New Zealand are tied together by and expressed at a cultural level through the organization of gender relations.

Footrot Flats: Expressing a Gendered Culture

Although *Footrot Flats* is a fiction of mythical proportions, its protagonists embody the dynamics of male and female cultures in New Zealand. For instance, the Dog and Cheeky Hobson not only represent masculine and feminine qualities, but their relationship epitomizes the struggle between male and female cultures which characterizes New Zealand life.

Who is Darleen (or Cheeky) Hobson? In the Dog's eyes, she's the:

... blonde barber who owns the La Parisienne Beauty Salon in Raupo. More dangerous than Sweeny Todd she's after Wal with her bitch-box eyes and her wagging tail. She shall not have him. She may have a fat chest but can she muster the bush paddock? (Ball, 1986.)

Even such a brief description exposes the contradictions within our gendered culture. Here the conflict between male mateship, a comradeship forged in labour and play, and heterosexual relations is laid bare. Mating is seen as inevitably absorbing men's agenda and culture into a feminine agenda and culture. The struggle between the male world of mateship and the female world of kinship surfaces repeatedly.

All the females in *Footrot Flats* are relatives, or in Cheeky Hobson's case, a potential relative, of Wal, the heroic farmer, or of Cooch, his mate. These kinship relations present direct threats to the relationships between the male figures: the Dog, Wal, and Cooch. Cheeky Hobson is the most obvious example. Her potential corruption of Wal is the site of direct struggle between the Dog and Cheeky. However, Wal's Aunt Dolly, too, while not offering the attractions of the flesh, imposes a feminine order on the masculine disorder of *Footrot Flats.* She is determined to bring civilization to Raupo with her city 'cats-home-ways', her unmentionable names for the Dog, and her sheer strength of will. Although Cooch's cousin, Kathy, along with Jess (the bitch), epitomizes a 'good' woman, she brings disruption to the masculine world by turning mates into competitors and men into thumb-sucking acolytes. Even Cooch, the perfect example of all that is 'best' in masculinity, becomes an opponent for the Dog when he locks Jess away in the bitch's box.

Deeply embedded in this cultural conscience is the notion that the masculine world is fragile, that women can destroy men's culture by overcoming it directly and by surreptitiously leading men into betraying their mates. Aunt Dolly not only dictates terms, she can actually buy the Dog and Wal off with her pikelets and the very civilizing services they fear and deride. Cheeky Hobson already has Wal's hormones under control, at least according to the Dog, but these are not her only attractions. The Dog himself is not immune to Cheeky Hobson. She gives him the home comforts that his mate Wal denies. Thus, the masculine world of hard yakker, play, and mates is constantly under threat from the 'soft' options and attractions which are represented and provided by women.

In *Footrot Flats,* as in everyday life in New Zealand, the divisions based on class and race[1] exist, but remain largely unexpressed. Where they do appear, the problems of race and class are minor, hardly distinguishable sub-plots subsumed under the problem of gender. Class divisions, for instance, are portrayed as a component of female culture.

The corgi, Prince Charles, might represent inequalities of class, but it was Aunt Dolly who brought him to Raupo. It is Aunt Dolly, too, who protects him from the republican egalitarian tendencies of Wal and the Dog, giving him rewards far in excess of his utilitarian value. Class is thus associated with pretentions to status, rather than power and control, and women are the primary bulwarks of pretention.

Pongo, the privately schooled, city-living niece of Wal is also associated with class. However, she is accepted as a mate by local boy Rangi and the Dog. Their relationship is broken only by Pongo's occasional uppityness. At these moments, the 'cultivated' behaviour which characterizes both femininity and the private school come together to humiliate and frustrate the authority of masculinity. Cousin Kathy and Jess are the female characters who escape this association. They may cause consternation by apparently favouring males other than Cooch and the Dog, but they never make a man feel uncouth.

Being mates is presented in New Zealand as fundamentally egalitarian. Male culture has no space for divisions of class and race. Rangi, the kid who idolizes Wal, tolerates Pongo, and is regarded by the Dog as a junior comrade, represents mateship between Māori and Pākehā men. Being sports mad and 'quite good at footy', Rangi wins the Dog's approval. Rangi is very much concerned with the manly pursuits of the sports field and outdoor life. His masculinity is developed, tested, and compared in these domains. His awareness of himself as a male in relation to women only surfaces in brief interludes. At times, he shows a precocious interest in Cheeky's voluptuous charms. More often, when Rangi is forced to acknowledge women in response to Pongo's assertion of her femininity or feminism, he merely dismisses women as a hindrance.

Race, as an issue, only appears in the midst of struggles between Rangi and Pongo as potential members of two different gender cultures. It is when Pongo succeeds at some 'masculine' activity and 'gets one up' on Rangi that he calls her a 'Pākehā'. Pongo lives in the masculine world of male mateship on borrowed time, and thus, while accepted as a participant, she must not excel in mateship activities. This is always a struggle, for Pongo is portrayed as having as much naturally endowed skill as Rangi. This, then, is a struggle over the boundaries and their rigidity, between masculine and feminine cultures, and the degree of access women and men have to each.

We have focused on *Footrot Flats* because the complex relations between the characters expose the real preoccupation New Zealanders have with the problem of gender. Gender shapes the way in which divisions and inequalities can be acknowledged and defined, not as social constructions and inequalities, but as natural cultural tendencies among men and women. By emphasizing the friendship and common interests or concerns among men, the gendered culture facilitates the maintenance of the egalitarian ethos which is characteristic of New Zealand life.

Although inequalities of class and race are seen daily in New Zealand, this is successfully countered by our society's egalitarian ethos. This ethos denotes not equality of position or outcome, but equality of opportunity. It is a view of society in which all are equally eligible to compete for society's rewards, irrespective of their birth or social position. The availability of this opportunity means that it is up to individuals to achieve. Such an understanding of equality is quite compatible with visible inequalities. It reinforces the idea that those inequalities are due to an individual's character or activities, not to the organization of social life (Oxley, 1978: 44-6; Pearson and Thorns, 1983: 239).

Distinguishing Sex and Gender

The primary preoccupation with gender is characteristic of a gendered culture, but the social construction of gender itself is a universal phenomenon among human societies. The concept of *gender* refers to qualities, traits, and activities collectively deemed to be masculine or feminine in any particular society. Although 'things feminine' are associated with females, and 'things masculine' are associated with males, sex and gender are quite distinct. The *content* of masculinity and femininity does not have an immediate biological foundation, despite the fact that gender defines what it means to be a male or female in a social sense. Gender is a categorization based not on physiological but on social attributes. Sex, that is the categories 'female' and 'male', is purely physiological. It refers to biological attributes which for the vast majority of the population can be simply ascertained by observing the nature of individuals' reproductive sex characteristics. Individuals may be born female or male but they have to *become* masculine or feminine. Societies socialize their members into gender roles and expectations and they associate various traits and qualities with gender categories. The very fact that these roles, expectations, traits, and qualities vary from society to society and over time, indicates the real but often hidden disjunction between sex and gender (Oakley, 1972).

All societies engage in the social construction of gender. Moreover, there appears to be a marked tendency for masculinity, whatever its content, to be rewarded more highly than activities and qualities associated with femininity (Rosaldo, 1980). Therefore, inequalities between those of the female sex and those with male physiology also tend to be a phenomenon of human societies.

In some societies, like New Zealand, the distinction between sex and gender is popularly ignored. Inequalities between women and men are commonly, though not scientifically, explained as deriving from a biological (sex-connected) superiority on the part of men. In other societies, such as the Mundurucú Indian society in South America, women are not seen as inferior because of their biology, but because their roles are inferior (Murphy and Murphy, 1985: 136). Popular understanding in Mundurucú society clearly distinguishes between sex and gender and, furthermore, asserts that the hierarchical relationship between men and women is mutable.

Defining a Gendered Culture

A gendered culture does not necessarily refer to cultures which are male dominated, or to those in which no popular distinction is made between sex and gender. If these were the characteristics of a gendered culture, many societies could be classified as such. Rather, we define a gendered culture as a culture in which all social relations are structured and understood through a prism of gender relations, through concepts of masculinity and femininity. Within a gendered culture, there exists distinct male and female cultures which, although integral to each other, are rigidly bounded. Consequently, the relations between men and women are highly ritualized and the assumption of masculinity and femininity and entry into the appropriate culture are the problems which dominate social relations. In essence, then, a gendered culture is one in which masculinity and femininity structure, express, and make sense of, at a popular level, the conflicts, interests, and inequalities which are integral to a society.

Like New Zealand, Mundurucú society is a gendered culture because every aspect of social relations is suffused and shaped by understandings of masculinity and femininity and the male and female cultures which arise around them. In Mundurucú society, women and men live in virtually separate worlds. Women sleep, socialize, play, and labour with women. Men engage in these activities with men. Consequently, the contacts between the sexes are ritualized and controlled. Men repeatedly assert their dominance over women, and while women privately ridicule such claims, they rarely publicly challenge male authority. To do so would invite ritual rape (Murphy and Murphy, 1985: 133).

Even in the mythology which Mundurucú Indians use to explain their existence as a society, there is embedded the problem of assuming masculinity or femininity and the struggle between male and female cultures. According to myth, women were the rulers of Mundurucú society in primeval times. Men had to overthrow women's rule in order to gain their autonomy. Just as in New Zealand, men seem to fear that the women's world will absorb and destroy men's relations with each other (Phillips, 1987: 257), Mundurucú men are apprehensive of a women's counter-revolution which would see men enslaved to women in the same way that women are presently subordinated to men (Murphy and Murphy, 1985: 116).

On the other hand, British society cannot be characterized as a gendered culture. Nevertheless, there are major inequalities between women and men which are rationalized by reference to concepts of masculinity and femininity very like those in New Zealand. However, gender is not the preoccupation of that society; gender is not its motif. The problematical nature of relations between women and men occupy the British just as the problems of race and class arise in the everyday lives of Pākehā in New Zealand. But in Britain, gender does not dominate. Instead, images of class suffuse British life. As John Betjeman observes of British society:

A single topic occupies our minds.
'Tis hinted at or boldly blazoned in our accents,
clothes and ways of eating fish,
And being introduced and taking leave,
'Farewell', 'So long', 'Bunghosky', 'Cheeribye'
That topic all — absorbing, as it was,
It is now and ever shall be, to us — CLASS. (Cited in Furbank, 1985: 4.)

The problem of assuming a position and style of a class is as preoccupying in Britain as the assumption of masculinity and femininity is in New Zealand. Just as gender cultures are in New Zealand regarded as natural, class cultures, though problematical, are regarded as natural in Britain (Gallie, 1983). In Britain, masculinity and femininity become part of the expression of class. Britain, then, unlike Mundurucú society and New Zealand society, is not, we suggest, a gendered culture. Some societies, of course, are neither absorbed by the notion of gender nor of class. South Africa, for instance, is a society in which inequalities of class and sex are shaped by a racist culture. The cultural expression of that preoccupation is apartheid (Parkin, 1979: 93-4).

Sexual inequalities in a gendered culture are not necessarily greater than in societies which are not gendered cultures. Nor are gendered cultures ones in which other divisions and inequalities are minor or non-existent. To understand a gendered culture, we cannot reduce it to the dynamics of sex inequalities. In New Zealand, there exist inequalities of race, class, and sex. These have distinct material connections, but they do not derive from each other. In other words, neither sex, nor class, nor race alone can be seen as the primary or determining structure of inequality in our society[2]. Indeed, it will be demonstrated that the gendered culture which developed in New Zealand, and is expressed so completely in *Footrot Flats,* emerged not merely out of sex struggle but also out of interests of race and class in the early colonial period.

Culture as a Way of Life

It should be noted that our concept of culture differs significantly from the way in which culture is commonly used. Generally, 'culture' refers to such activities as the arts and literature. Sometimes, distinctions and preferences are made between 'high' and 'low' culture. High culture includes such pursuits as opera, ballet, and the type of visual and literary arts which are seen as the most sophisticated and systematic expressions of the 'Human Spirit'. In contrast, low culture refers to popular music, literature, and art designed for mass consumption. Because high culture is identified with civilization, this view of culture invariably identifies cultural activities with the élite. Low culture is merely the 'uncouth utterances of the people'.

Among some sociologists, culture is used in an alternative way. They reject the division of culture into 'high' or 'low' and the associated devaluation of popular culture. Instead of defining popular culture as the unsophisticated expression of crude lives, they celebrate popular culture as complex attempts by non-élite groups both to make sense of their 'world' and to resist domination by the politically and socially powerful (Jones, 1984). In this context, culture is used when referring to 'shared principles of life, characteristics of particular classes, groups or shared social milieux' (Griffin, 1985: 202). Within any society, a myriad of cultures exist because culture refers to systems of ideas, symbols, preferences, and expressions.

While we too recognize that culture is not only created by dominant groups, our view of culture is a more inclusive one. Culture embraces both symbolic expression and the structural relations which delimit everyday life. Culture consists of: 'the total lifestyle of a people . . . all of the ideas, knowledge, behaviour and material objects that they share' (Sullivan and Thompson, 1984: 35).

In summary, then, cultures have dominant motifs which ultimately structure the practises associated with different groups. In Britain, the culture is dominated by a class motif. In New Zealand, as in the Mundurucú society, it is a gender motif. While subordinated groups, such as Polynesians, women, and working-class people in our society, may engage in resistances against dominant élites, they do so within an overall cultural framework. In that framework, there are distinct male and female cultures which together constitute our gendered culture.

A Critical Analysis of Our Gendered Culture

In New Zealand, a certain type of masculinity and femininity structures the practices and symbols of our society, and in doing so, throws up real and immediate social problems: violence; domestic and sexual abuse; impoverishment; human wastage on the roads; alcohol abuse; and psychiatric illness. All are associated with the dynamics of male and female cultures in New Zealand. Our concern is to confront these problems, and, more importantly, expose the connections between them and the inequalities of class, race, and sex which systematically divide our society. These social problems which come out of the gendered culture impose costs on all members of our society. They demand the intervention of the State and the expenditure of social and economic resources. Such expenditures have created much public controversy over the last decade, but rarely has the gendered culture itself been challenged. We shall consider why this is the case.

The costs of these social problems fall particularly hard on those who are excluded from the ownership of productive property, Māori, Pacific Islanders, and women. Moreover, these costs are largely accepted, in part, because the gendered culture is popularly perceived as natural and immutable. More importantly, such acceptance reflects the significant role a gendered culture plays within our society in managing conflicts of class, race, and sex, particularly to the benefit of élites based on class, race, and sex.

During the course of this book, we examine the origins, structures, and dynamics of a gendered culture and critique its place in New Zealand society. Our gendered culture emerged out of the exigencies of Britain's colonization of Aotearoa. It was not an import to this country, nor was it part of Māori indigenous culture. Rather it developed as a means to cope with the continuous struggles over land, which was the productive base of early colonial society. These struggles were not just between Māori and Pākehā, but were among the Pākehā, between propertied and unpropertied, and between men and women. The conflicts between these social actors threw up social disorders and problems which, by the end of the nineteenth century, required a collective societal response. This response was the elaboration of particular forms of femininity and masculinity and their organization into distinct female and male cultures. Female culture was constituted through the 'Cult of Domesticity'. Its embodiment of such qualities as nurturance, morality, and domesticity, we shall argue, was crucial in the State's response to social disruption in the late nineteenth century. Male culture, as we shall see, was somewhat more ambiguous. It both contributed to the problems confronting the New Zealand State and provided solutions to it. Male culture integrated two apparently contradictory constructions: the 'Man Alone' and the 'Family Man'.

Male and female cultures are still structured through the Man Alone/Family Man and the Cult of Domesticity today. However, the interface between those cultures and their substance has somewhat altered. Moreover, they are not so completely accepted in contemporary times, particularly as the costs associated with them are increasingly apparent. After considering the contemporary practices of our gendered culture, we outline the individual and societal costs with which it is associated. We must then confront the major question of why, despite the enormous costs of a gendered culture, it is so rarely challenged at an institutional level and, frequently, so avidly supported. We discuss the nature of vested interests in that culture and the extent to which these are associated with the systematic maintenance of the inequalities of class, race, and sex in New Zealand. In the light of this, we finally suggest that it is imperative for those whose ultimate interests lie in a more equal and more just society to recognize their collective material interests in dismantling the gendered culture in New Zealand.

1 In this book, we examine inequalities of race primarily in relation to Māori and Pākehā. The reason for this is that we argue that the gendered culture emerges out of the historical clash between the Māori as the indigenous people of Aotearoa and the British colonial settlers. Currently, relations between Māori and Pākehā are most significant and volatile in terms of race and ethnic relations in New Zealand (Spoonley, 1988). In particular, the Māori are regarded as experiencing and, by many Pākehā, as contributing to major social problems. We wish to locate this in the context of the development and continuing maintenance of a gendered culture.

2 At a theoretical level, the debate over the connections between inequalities of race, class, and sex has never been resolved. This, in part, is due to the tendency to assume that one structure of inequality must determine the rest. For example, that inequalities of class determine inequalities of sex and race (Bedggood, 1980), or that inequalities of sex determine race and class (Firestone, 1972) or that inequalities of race determine class and sex (Awatere, 1984). Our position is that this primacy debate is not a useful one, in that it focuses on the wrong level of abstraction. (See preface for elaboration.)

Race, Class, and Sex:
land and the struggle for power

The notions of masculinity and femininity embedded in New Zealand's gendered culture were brought to Aotearoa[1] by British migrants. The gendered culture itself, however, was not an import. The major preoccupation of the British, both at home and abroad, was not gender but the problem of determining individuals' appropriate 'station' according to differential access to property, skills, and occupation (Eldred-Grigg, 1977). The focus on the issue of gender, the development of distinct feminine and masculine cultures, and the creation of a culture in which the most intimate as well as structural expressions of social life are gender divided was a response to the exigencies of colonial life. New Zealand's gendered culture derived from a complex interaction between indigenous and colonial structures which met during the early period of colonization.

Everywhere, colonization is a process fraught with conflict. The transformation of Aotearoa into a British colony and its development as the settler society of New Zealand was no exception. However, conflict was not limited to a confrontation between Pākehā and the indigenous Māori society. Pākehā society itself was increasingly disturbed by conflicts of class and sex. All these conflicts were closely associated with the problem of access to, and rights over, land. Land provided the means of survival for everyone. Land was fundamental to Māori society, its availability inspired the migration of British people to the new colony, and it was land which formed the productive basis of the migrant household and structured relations between the sexes.

Given the vital connection between the land and traditional Māori society, it was virtually inevitable that the confrontation between Māori and Pākehā would be played out in that arena. Land was also central to the organization of relations between the sexes and between classes in Pākehā society. The relations which developed between Pākehā men and women were dependent on the ability of migrant households to be self-sufficient and the mutual reciprocity and dependency created under such circumstances. These household relations were potentially in conflict with the interests of the British bourgeoisie who chose to invest in and, sometimes, migrate to the new colony.

The successful pursuit of profit which prompted investment in New

Zealand was largely contingent on the control of large tracts of land. For the poor, however, the very attraction of the colony lay in its promise of acres of fertile and freely accessible land. Thus, interests regarding land access *within* Pākehā society were potentially opposed in the same way that Pākehā agrarian society was in conflict with traditional Māori resource uses. Land, then, became the pivot of three sets of structural relations in early colonial society; race, class, and sex. It is by no means coincidental that the Anglo-Māori Wars of the 1860s were accompanied by a significant struggle among the Pākehā over access to land, as well as a major breakdown in household self-sufficiency and associated exchanges between women and men.

Land Struggles Between Māori and Pākehā

When British settlers came to Aotearoa, they came to a country with well-established customs of land tenure and usage. These were based on rights and obligations associated with kinship. Claims to land were activated and proven through lineages in which descent was traced not only through the male but the female lines (Firth, 1973: 385-6; Kawharu, 1977: 294). Thus, land, kinship, and individual identity were united for the Māori.

Land was the ancestral home of the kin group and each individual's connection with it was expressed through the burial of their placenta and umbilical cord. Similarly, the meeting house, the centre of the community decision making and ceremony, was typically named after a significant ancestor and represented his or her body. Land embodied the present, the past, and the future (Sinclair, 1975).

The land was of great economic, spiritual, cultural, and symbolic importance to the Māori. It was the economic base of their society. An area would involve complex claims to the use of its resources: for example, the right to snare birds, catch eel and fish, and to cultivate plants (Firth, 1973: 379). The Māori added other economic uses of land according to the trade opportunities presented by Pākehā settlements:

... for a Maori, ... the European market economy allowed new opportunities for mana and competition; and these developments were largely not unwelcomed. (Asher and Naulls, 1987: 11.)

The Māori enthusiastically embraced the new European economic order and skilfully competed within it. With a communal style of farming unaffected by rising labour costs (Miller, 1974: 134), Māori food production soon became the mainstay of New Zealand Company settlements and settlements around Auckland. The Māori also exported

agricultural produce to the Californian and Victorian gold-fields
(Sorrenson, 1984: 172). Some tribes ran highly successful commercial
ventures including flour mills and fleets of trading vessels (Howe, 1977:
28). These Māori economic activities were essential both to the colony's
agricultural production and the raising of Government revenue.

In 1856, the Māori population contributed almost half of the customs
revenue. Furthermore, profits from the sale of Māori land made up three-
quarters of the colonial Government's land fund:

It would not be unfair to say that the Maori population of New Zealand both
fed the settlers and paid many of their public bills. (Simpson, 1979: 112.)

But, for many reasons, the Māori's economic dominance declined. Their
initial advantages in collective farming were overcome by the less
sophisticated British system of individual land tenure which gave
Pākehā access to credit and greater opportunity to use technology
(Sorrenson, 1984: 172). Where the Pākehā could appropriate enough
land in the South Island, the Wairarapa, and Hawke's Bay, they developed
profitable pastoral farming.

The development of pastoral farming placed the burgeoning
Pākehā population in direct competition with the Māori for land. After
1840, acquiring land for both occupation and as capital investment
became the primary concern of the Pākehā. Between 1843 and 1860,
the Pākehā population increased sevenfold (Asher and Naulls, 1987: 14),
dramatically reversing the ratio of settlers to indigenous people. The
flow of settlers into the colony was encouraged by the British
Government precisely because Aotearoa offered a vast amount of land
which could absorb Britain's surplus population of rural and urban poor.
Revenue from the sale of land obtained from the Māori in the colony
was used to finance assisted immigrant schemes (Steven, 1985: 42-3).

Compared to the Māori, British settlers had an equally strong,
although different, vision of the land. This was not simply a difference
between a Māori spiritual affinity with the land, as opposed to an entirely
instrumental Pākehā attitude. The main difference lay in the basis of
land tenure itself. For the Māori, ownership of land was not conceived
of in individual terms. It involved rights of resource access, occupation,
and cultivation in common with other members of the kin group and
according to the chief's decisions. 'The land was regarded as a sacred
trust and asset of the people as a whole,' (Sinclair, 1975: 116). In contrast,
the Pākehā viewed land as meeting individual requirements and tenure
determined within the framework of legal regulation.

Māori communal concepts of land did not prevent its sale.
Nevertheless, to the Māori the meaning of sale was different from that
assumed by the Pākehā. To some Māori chiefs, the sale of land merely

indicated the granting of rights of occupancy to the Pākehā. Far from seeing the sale of land as ceding eternally their rights to land, some Māori used the sale of land to assert their claim to it (Asher and Naulls, 1987: 15-16). Land sales promised the Māori power and prosperity because it facilitated the holding of European goods.

After the Treaty of Waitangi, Pākehā settlers were legally bound to buy land from the Crown or its agents rather than from the Māori. This led to increasing frustration among settlers and culminated in Pākehā agitation for self-government, independent from the British Colonial Office. Self-government would give settlers the power to acquire land directly from the Māori (Miller, 1974: 156).

For the Crown, its buying and selling of land were essential to make the colony viable. From 1840, the Crown appropriated land through legislation designed to protect the Māori from land speculators and to facilitate the orderly transfer of land to Pākehā. The sale of these lands by the Crown to settlers was used to finance the new colony. The Colonial Office in London was determined that New Zealand and its other colonies would be self-supporting and 'was not to become. . . that greatest of all evils — a charge on the British taxpayer' (Gardner, 1984: 59).

Land purchase was particularly successful in the South Island where Kai Tahu, who held the largest territory in the country, was divested of its land. While southern colonial pastoralists prospered, Kai Tahu were reduced to penury on reserves. They were denied land to undertake competitive pastoral farming and were separated from their traditional sources of food (Evison, 1986: 32).

In the North Island, the Māori retained control over the fertile Waikato area which was a hub of agricultural production in the colony, and Pākehā land agents and prospective farmers in Auckland sought to obtain this land (Simpson, 1979: 136). However, many Māori were discontented with the Crown's practice of buying land cheaply and selling it at enormous profits. Increasingly, Māori felt their control over land sales to be slipping away:

What began as a willingness to sell land that seemed surplus to tribal requirements turned into a deepening suspicion of growing Pakeha power and land hunger. . . (Asher and Naulls, 1987: 21.)

In Taranaki and the Waikato, some Māori tribes placed a tapu on the land in an effort to prevent sale. The Kingitanga, a Waikato confederation of tribes, most vehemently resisted land sales. Such movements, dubbed 'anti-land selling leagues' by the Pākehā, raised the strongest reaction. To the settlers, it seemed as if the Māori were, if not illegally, then at

least unethically, uniting to exclude Pākehā from land ownership
(Simpson, 1979: 124).

The Crown's authority as sole land buyer, which was increasingly
challenged by both Māori and Pākehā settlers, was further undermined
by its own land purchase agents. By the mid-1850s, agents commonly
made deals with individual Māori to sell land without the permission
of kin. According to Simpson (1979: 116), these events were instrumental
in precipitating the wars which erupted in 1859 at Waitara when troops
moved against Māori obstructing a land surveying party. Soon the
fighting spread to the Waikato, as the colonial Government endeavoured
to break the Kingitanga.

The wars were not simply over land. They epitomized the struggle
between Pākehā and Māori for control over the country and the new
society. The wars resulted in the confiscation of large areas of fertile
land suitable for agriculture in the Waikato, Taranaki, Bay of Plenty,
and Gisborne areas, irrespective of tribal involvement in the wars. These
confiscations are still bitterly resented today (see Awatere, 1984). Much
of the land was sold by the Crown and that which was returned was
clearly considered to be the least valuable.

The loss of land meant the collapse of Māori society. Confined to
the infertile areas, they were transformed into a marginal rural proletariat.
The Māori existed on the edges of Pākehā society, largely without
political influence and denied economic autonomy. This ensured the
economic, political, and cultural dominance of the Pākehā over the
Māori.

Class Struggles Over Land Among Pākehā

Pākehā as a whole benefited from the taking of Māori land. The pressure
on the remnants of Māori land during the 1860s, however, represented
not merely a struggle between Māori and Pākehā. It reflected a class
struggle within Pākehā society which was disrupting the fragile early
colonial social order. The confiscation of Māori land by the Crown after
the Anglo-Māori Wars was as much an attempt to defuse the discontent
of the growing numbers of Pākehā landless as it was to impose British
sovereignty finally in Aotearoa or even to satisfy the demands of
Pākehā land speculators.

British immigrants came to Aotearoa in the 1840s and 1850s, bringing
with them a vision of a classless society. This was not, however, a
rejection of inequality. By the 1820s in Britain, the word 'class' had
become associated not merely with inequality, but with the systematic
exploitation of certain sections of the community by others (Furbank,

1985: 5-6). The attempt to establish a 'classless' society in New Zealand represented a repudiation of this and the notions of 'class interests' and 'class conflicts' with which it was connected. It was a restatement of the 'naturalness' of social inequality.

New Zealand seemingly provided an opportunity to re-establish the idea of mutual dependency, exchange, and respect between those of different 'stations'. For the gentry, New Zealand was a haven from the apparent menace of working-class organization and tensions in Britain (Hamer, 1965: 80). For Britain's new poor, New Zealand held the promise of a higher station. Perhaps more importantly, it offered an opportunity to reassert traditional rights of control over work and the means of survival which had been wrested from them by the onslaught of new industrial divisions of labour (Pahl, 1984: 41-57).

Early colonial New Zealand became an agricultural society dominated by independent producers with 'most labourers probably expecting to own their own farms and often buying subsistence farms within village boundaries' (Olssen, 1977: 30). Even among the Wakefield settlements, in which the New Zealand Company pursued a policy of separating capital and labour by restricting land to those with capital, the exigencies of colonial settlement meant that labourers were eventually given vacant land on which to develop subsistence farms (Gardner, 1984: 61). This development did not satisfy absentee British landowners, who had hoped for a rapid return on their investments through land speculation, but without it, the colony would have collapsed.

Early colonial society was marked by subsistence production, a social order characterized by gently graduated differences of status, reciprocity, and paternalistic self-regulation with socio-economic interests mediated by shared community institutions (Graham, 1984: 119-20; Olssen and Levesque, 1978: 2-3). It was a society in which inequalities, both social and economic, were deeply embedded and seen not as oppositional and exploitative but as mutually beneficial. The fragility of such a world was exposed by the boom which accompanied the Victorian gold-rush in the late 1850s.

Apart from being a potent attraction for labourers in New Zealand, the gold-rushes created an unprecedented demand for agricultural produce. This had a contradictory effect on small farmers and potential landholders with limited access to capital. The diversification of the export market from wool to other products gave subsistence farmers access to capital from which they had previously been excluded. On the other hand, new investment opportunities in agriculture brought a boom to the land market which raised land prices to heights prohibitive to most migrants. This was compounded by a shortage of unencumbered land. Kai Tahu may have lost much of their land in the South Island but large tracts of land in the North were under tribal control. Moreover, land under Pākehā ownership was increasingly monopolized by a few.

The pastoralists' monopolization of land available to the Pākehā had caused concern since the late 1840s. In 1853, Governor Grey imposed 50-75 per cent reductions on the price of rural lands in a misguided attempt to improve the ability of other less well-endowed migrants to buy agricultural property. The result was a further consolidation of land by the wealthy (Gardner, 1984: 64). The exclusion of much of the rapidly increasing Pākehā population from secure access to viable landholdings was accompanied by the progressive impoverishment of those reliant on subsistence agriculture. Together, these provided the basis of rural struggle which underpinned social relations in New Zealand throughout the middle of the nineteenth century (Olssen, 1977: 27).

The monopoly control of land gave pastoralists enormous economic, political, and social power (Fairburn, 1979: 55-60). However, monopolization itself actually posed a threat to the continuation of that power. Between the 1860s and the 1880s, a rural itinerant Pākehā population, which flooded the urban areas and roamed the countryside, came to be regarded as a major social problem. The breakdown in communal control that this reflected was accelerated by fluctuating demands for wage labour. The gold-rushes, Vogel's public works in the 1870s, and the later boom of urban industry all collapsed, leaving those without capital with the prospect of destitution. The vision of New Zealand as a stable hierarchical society based on mutual obligations disappeared.

Notwithstanding the development of the urban-based worker and associated instances of industrial disorder, class struggle expressed a central concern with the problem of land distribution and access. Right up until the twentieth century, trade union leaders were committed to the notion that urban and rural wage and salary earners should have access, as of right, to land (Fairburn, 1979: 56). Over one and a half million acres of land in the North Island were made available to the Pākehā by the Crown's confiscation of lands after the Anglo-Māori Wars (Sorrenson, 1984: 185). It was this land, as much as that which was later made available by the breakdown of the South Island pastoral estates, which allowed the New Zealand Government to pursue various land-settlement schemes over the subsequent century. These schemes were aimed at placing individuals, and more particularly families, with small amounts of capital on the land.

The property ambitions of the Pākehā in New Zealand may have been progressively reduced to owning merely an urban section and house, but widespread land ownership has had a pronounced impact on class identity in New Zealand. Few New Zealanders own land in any quantity.

Even in 1891, while possibly as many as 29 per cent of the wage- and salary-earning male population were freeholders, 42 per cent of improved land value was in the hands of 1.3 per cent of the freeholding population (Fairburn, 1979: 57). Similarly, in the late 1970s, while some 69 per cent of householders in New Zealand were owner-occupiers, the vast proportion of land area and value was controlled by relatively few private or State corporations (Pearson and Thorns, 1983: 67). Despite the consolidation of land in the hands of a few, the wide spread of land ownership has been cited as underpinning the conservative nature of New Zealand society, the persistence of myths of egalitarianism and the lack of class identity (Pearson and Thorns, 1983: 63-71). If this is so, the effective obscuring of class interests, conflicts, and boundaries has been achieved, in part, through the alienation of the Māori from their land resource (Steven, 1985).

Pressure from small farmers and agricultural labourers in both the pastoral ruling class and the colonial State, combined with the pastoralists' own interests in expansion and the speculative interests of urban-based businessmen, were all instrumental in bringing about the Anglo-Māori Wars and subsequent land confiscations. Class conflicts not only became transformed into racial conflicts, but changes in the structural relations betweeen Māori and Pākehā were used to resolve class struggles within Pākehā society.

The common element which allowed such a transformation was land. Within the structures of class and race relations in early colonial New Zealand, it was the control of land which was the foundation for power. It was also the foundation of the relationship between Pākehā women and men. Here, too, the crisis of the 1860s which changed the meaning and value of land had a profound economic and social impact.

The Collapse of the Colonial Household: land and sex conflict

Poor communications and transport made self-sufficiency a necessity for Pākehā settler households. They had to grow their own food, butcher their own meat, make bread, soap, and clothing (Miller, 1974: 132-4). Women played a considerable role in maintaining the household's self-sufficiency. For women, the division of labour between the sexes was flexible. They would turn their hand to any work required in the house or on the farm (Pahl, 1984: 18-62). So valuable was the contribution of the colonial wife that prospective male migrants were advised by British immigration agencies that 'an extra week spent in looking for a wife would be more advantageous than buying a patent plough or a thoroughbred horse' (Graham, 1984: 124).

Women arrived with husbands or as domestic servants with the full expectation of quick marriages. They had come to a colony where there was a considerable surplus of men to women. In 1851 the first census recorded a sex ratio of 776 Pākehā women for every 1,000 Pākehā men (Phillips, 1987: 6). The scarcity of single women inflated their 'market value' as wives and as employees, much to the chagrin of the gentry who constantly complained about the lack of domestic staff and the high wages they could command (Miller, 1974: 126). Women's work and familial roles were oriented towards the maintenance of the household as a whole. The household was not at this time, as it was to become, the emotional refuge from the world of competitive production. It was, instead, the site of production. Thus, women were not so much providers of psychological and material support for men, but, rather, participants in the household's overall productive capacity. Men were dependent on women's and children's labour.

During the period in which the colonial household was the dominant site of production and reproduction, Pākehā women had few legal rights. Married women were legally subordinate to their husbands in both the sphere of production and reproduction. Until the 1884 Married Women's Property Act, Pākehā married women had virtually no right to own, control, or dispose of property. Husbands owned all familial property, even property originally brought into a marriage by the wife. It was by no means unusual for deserting husbands to take with them all the family's assets (Koopman–Boyden and Scott, 1984: 104–5). This became increasingly frequent in the 1860s and 1870s when depressed wages and unpredictable employment opportunities for men made the support of dependants difficult. The 1884 Act allowed married women to treat their rights over their own property as an estate separate from their husband's interests.

Husbands also controlled the reproductive and sexual lives of their wives. The conjugal rights of husbands were, and remained until very recently, sacrosanct. While the 1867 divorce law allowed men to divorce their wives on the grounds of adultery, women could only divorce their husbands on grounds of adultery combined with violence (Phillips, 1987: 18). Moreover, men, whatever the grounds of divorce, received custody of any children. Fathers had the 'sole ownership and responsibility for their children' (Koopman–Boyden and Scott, 1984: 104–6, 198). Pākehā women's access to abortion was very restricted. It was not until 1893, the same year that Pākehā women gained a political voice for the first time, that abortion to save the mother's life was legalized (Koopman–Boyden and Scott, 1984: 115). In short, Pākehā women, within Pākehā society, were denied the rights of citizenship which pertained to men.

They were defined, like children, as minors.

It is difficult to assess the degree to which Pākehā gender relations were imposed on the gender relations of the Māori in the early years of colonization. Māori women were governed by the laws of colonial society which left them in the same position as Pākehā women. Nevertheless, the Māori strove to maintain their own customs, and in reality, where there was cohabitation, such families tended to live in Māori rather than European style (Sorrenson, 1984: 170). In any case Māori-Pākehā marriages were uncommon in colonial New Zealand (Eldred-Grigg, 1984: 19) and, consequently, most Māori women's gender experience was determined by a social structure and world view quite different to that of the Pākehā.

Because traditional Māori society was predominantly stratified according to age and genealogy, Māori women of high rank appear to have had power and influence in a number of spheres from which their Pākehā counterparts were excluded. Nevertheless, there is some debate. Best (1974: 99-100), in his account of pre-colonial Māori society, which was mainly based on his contact with the Tuhoe people, emphasized that Māori women were regarded as inferior to men. They had to do all of the domestic work, much of the procuring of food supplies, and, in Best's opinion, 'far too much heavy work'. However, Best, like other commentators, also observed that some women of high-ranking families had gained commanding positions. There are numerous examples of such women. Makereti, born in 1872, was a women of exceptionally high rank within the Arawa tribe. Her sex did not prevent her from taking on the full responsibilities and mana expected of a person of her rank. As *te aho ariki,* Makereti was the first born of the most senior line: 'In her came together the lines of all the chiefs and learned and sacred tohunga. . .' (Penniman, in Makereti, 1986: 20). Being of such illustrious lineage, Makereti was singled out by her elders to be taught her people's history and geneology, that is, the sacred knowledge of her people, '. . .and all the duties that she would be called upon to perform in life' (Penniman, in Makereti, 1986: 20).

Rose Pere (1982: 49), of Tuhoe and Ngati Kahungunu, comments that the most senior women of the whānau were responsible for passing on knowledge of the environment and resources. Women, as well as men, would be chosen to attend the higher institutions of learning for rangatira. Pere (1982: 51-2) is adamant that women were highly respected. Her female Māori forebears:

. . .were extremely liberated as compared to the author's English tipuna. With the exception of slaves (male and female) the women were never regarded as chattels or possessions; they retained their own names at marriage. Retaining their own identity and whakapapa (genealogy) was one of the utmost importance

and children could identify with the kinship group of either or both parents. . .
Assault, which could have included rape or an insult to women, involved a
penalty of death or some very severe punishment for the offender.

Māori women were heavily involved in production as Best himself
pointed out. Like Pākehā women, Māori women made a major
contribution to the subsistence of their whānau through their work in
food production by gathering food, helping in cultivation, and taking
rats from runs (Best, 1974: 99–100; Makereti, 1986: 157–253;). Most
significantly, Māori women had well-established rights to land and
associated water resources (Kawharu, 1977: 49). Indeed they had similar
privileges to men (Kawharu, 1977: 295). Furthermore, unlike Pākehā
women, Māori women controlled their reproduction, making the
decisions concerning conception and contraception, abortion and
infanticide (Gluckman, 1976: 174, 184, 188).

Just as Māori women appeared to have a self-determining role in
sexual matters, they also had a significant political role in Māori society.
There are many examples of powerful women leaders, especially among
the Ngati Porou (Mahuika, 1975), but not exclusively. While women
may not have been permitted to stand and speak on the marae itself in
many tribes, they were nevertheless able to engage in public debate
within the meeting house (Salmond, 1976: 45). Furthermore, women
wielded, and still do wield, an influence on the marae itself through
their role as supporters to the male orators. Salmond (1976: 127) observed
many contemporary instances of women carrying out 'corrective action'
when a male speaker overstepped marae protocol. If he spoke too long,
or he became overly boring, the kuia (female elders) would signal their
displeasure by making pointed comments, and, in the last resort, stand
up to sing his song, thus effectively silencing him. The ultimate
opprobrium, of presenting one's backside to the offender of custom,
is most often done by women (Salmond, 1976: 150, 151). Such gestures
are ways in which Māori women had, and still retain in contemporary
ceremonial sittings, a public power. Moreover, women of rank were able
to manifest and control spiritual power as tohunga.[2] Female prophets
were also prominent among the nineteenth century Māori Christian
millenarian movements, particularly among the Ringatu (Binney and
Chaplin, 1986: 25).

Perhaps the most striking contrast between the position of women
in Māori and Pākehā societies was to do with mana.[3] In Māori society
it was not unusual for the hapū (kin group) to be named after a
prominent woman ancestor (Mahuika, 1975). Nowhere in Pākehā
society could women embody so completely the prestige, power, and
identity of a group. On the contrary, Pākehā colonial society was

evolving a national and cultural ethos based on masculine characteristics forged in combat with nature:

To fell the forest giants, to dispel the gloom and mystery of the bush, to make the drear places beautiful and fruitful, to give wealth and productiveness to the land. There is warrior blood in the veins of the pioneer settlers. . . Theirs is not the life of ease and comfort. . . Theirs to fight and labour; theirs the blood and the spirit to live in the land and hold it when luxury has sapped the virility of the city-bred. (Cited in Phillips, 1980: 228.)

In the late nineteenth century, popular images of earlier pioneer society celebrated men's struggle with nature. However, the reality was that Pākehā women and men were virtually dependent on each other in this struggle. Their success was represented by the self-sufficient colonial household and a certain balance of power between men and women within it (Dalziel, 1986).

By the 1860s, the colonial household, based on subsistence production, was no longer dominant. Its viability had been undermined by pressures on the availability of land, and the attractions of wages which could be earned outside the household in gold-fields, public works, and urban industry. However, these wage-earning opportunities were primarily opportunities for men. This gave men independence and made women increasingly dependent. For Pākehā women, changes from a pioneer society to a more urban society meant a loss of the economic power associated with work in the self-sufficient household. This loss was not compensated for by access to wage labour because the opportunity for entry into paid production, except as very cheap labour, was extremely limited. By the 1880s, women, children, and the elderly were confronted with dire impoverishment as men shook off familial obligations.

Although working-class women were most profoundly affected by the disintegration of the colonial household and the threat of desertion, women's dependence and lack of civil rights posed a danger to the class system itself. Women's lack of property rights meant that marrying, and subsequently deserting, a middle-class woman represented a sound financial investment (Koopman-Boyden and Scott, 1984: 103). This, as much as the destitution of working-class women, was clearly in the minds of the pastoralists and businessmen of Parliament when they enacted the Married Women's Property Act.

In the early colonial period, the scarcity of women's labour and their labour value in the colonial household was associated with an ability to demand high rates of remuneration in paid work, particularly in domestic service. The later devaluation of women's productive labour in the household was subsequently accompanied by a disintegration of women's market power. In consequence, the conditions of women's employment became extremely exploitative.

Women were worst off in Dunedin and Christchurch where their conditions of work prompted a national inquiry into sweated labour. It is by no means coincidental that in these centres, the female population had far outstripped the male population (Olssen, 1980: 160). The exploitation of women's productive labour was accompanied by a sub-economy of prostitution which many women used to supplement their legitimate incomes. By 1893, it is estimated that Christchurch supported 280 full-time prostitutes, some 4 per cent of all women aged between fifteen and forty years. In Auckland, the proportion was higher with around 8 per cent of women in 1889 engaged in full-time prostitution (Eldred–Grigg, 1984: 39).

Desertion, destitution, and prostitution underpinned a burgeoning urban culture among the 'lower classes', which threatened the sanctity of private property and the social leadership of the professional middle classes and the landed gentry. Violence, drunkeness, gangs of street kids (larrikins), theft, gambling, and 'idleness' were endemic in the 1880s and 1890s (Olssen, 1984). The fragmentation of the colonial household had been accompanied by the disintegration of networks of social control.

The pioneer household was more than a site of production and reproduction. It was a mechanism of government. Through British common law, the State invested in men discretionary power over the family and its members. In return, patriarchal family heads administered social relations and sustained public order. Familial authority was indivisible from the authority relations of society as a whole. Where the family ruled, so too did the State. Where it did not, the State was confronted with the problem of preserving social order (Donzelot, 1979).

This problem could not be easily resolved. The State was caught between the expense of maintaining social order, either through welfare or coercion, and the problem of limiting fiscal expenditure. There was already a huge public debt and resistance to increased taxes from wealthy landowners, businessmen, and the professional middle classes. Thus, Government strategies were directed initially to restating the legal responsibility for welfare and social control on kin. 'Even at the beginning, however, a significant minority saw such strategies as both inappropriate and potentially ineffective. By 1877, the parliamentarian McKenzie argued that the State should intervene directly to 'take some charge of deserted children. . . and train them in such a way that they could not swell the criminal ranks' (cited in Koopman–Boyden and Scott, 1984: 101).

The State was forced to intervene because the potential social costs of non-intervention were so high. Some families simply could not support their kin, and some individuals had no kin at all. The State established laws to regulate children and parents (the Education Act in 1877) and granted civil rights which protected women's economic position (the Married Women's Property Act in 1884). It extended its own welfare support and provided funds to a variety of charitable institutions. Not only did these strategies all involve the State in expense, but they also could be seen as undermining male rights over women and children. While State welfare relieved men of some of the burden of their dependants, it also provided women with an instrument of resistance against male control and male violence. As one destitute mother commented to a prominent benefactor:

Do not send for my husband; we starve in peace when he is away, but we starve in misery when he is at home. (Tennant, 1986: 41.)

Two major contradictions emerged which spelt acute problems for the State by the mid-1880s. The first was the contradiction between the provision of welfare, and the State's already overstretched budget. The second was between the requirements of the State to control men and children, and the maintenance of male authority. Resolution of such contradictions involved the State in reinforcing the family in new ways. It emphasized the social control role of women as wives and mothers and, in doing so, set the context for the systematic expression of a gendered culture which has dominated New Zealand ever since.

The crisis which pervaded New Zealand society in the latter half of the nineteenth century was a crisis of sex, race, and class relations. Its expressions were diverse and apparently disparate. They ranged from the Anglo-Māori Wars of the 1860s to, as the century wore on, the increasing incidence of vagrancy, destitution, and the desertion of women, children, and elderly dependants by male kin. Struggles over political rights and responsibilities between the provinces and central Government, propertied and unpropertied, raged through the 1870s. They were dampened for a time by the abolition of provincial Government in 1876 and the extension of the franchise to unpropertied men in 1879, only to surface again over women's suffrage in the late 1880s and early 1890s. In the South Island, there were problems such as fire-raising, poaching, and sheep stealing. In the North Island, pockets of Māori resistance and millenial sects emerged. All Māori were faced with impoverishment, disease, and an alarming, seemingly irreversible, population decline. New Zealand society became a society of disorder rather than order.

This disorder emerged out of struggles over survival between the propertied and unpropertied, Pākehā and Māori, and men and women, respectively. By the mid nineteenth century, Pākehā men and the propertied had appropriated the traditional means of survival (land) and were progressively dominating the structure of urban-based production. It was not in the material interests of these groups to give up this control through the redistribution of land or the development of an inclusive and egalitarian labour market. On the other hand, the destitution and disruption created by the often contradictory interests of those dominant groups underpinned a social disorder which actually threatened their continued social and economic authority. Dominant élites were confronted with a particular problem: how could subordinate groups be given real, material incentives to retain a social order in which they had little ultimate control over the distribution of social and economic resources? The resolution of that problem involved a profound restructuring of material and ideological relations. The inequalities of class, sex, and race were subsumed, and the crises associated with them dissipated, by the creation of a gendered culture.

1 We use Aotearoa to refer to this country prior to European colonial rule. New Zealand is used to refer to contemporary society, because the use of Aotearoa would suggest a far greater recognition of Māori social and economic structures, political rights, and values than is now the case.

2 Tohunga — the traditional spiritual leaders and knowledge bearers of Māori society.

3 The concept 'mana' is difficult to translate into English. It involves the notions of power, influence, authority, and prestige, which are legitimated by members of the society. Mana is visited on high-ranking people but it can also be acknowledged in individuals of outstanding ability (Pere, 1982: 32).

Creating a Gendered Culture

The resolution of the social disorder characteristic of the mid to late nineteenth century involved a profound restructuring of material relations and popular understandings of the nature of New Zealand society. Central to this restructuring was the promotion of a strict sexual division of labour, the development of concepts of masculinity and femininity already latent in Pākehā society, and the association of masculine and feminine attributes with the 'national interest'. The State and popular discourse in New Zealand became focused almost entirely on the promotion of the 'Cult of Domesticity' and the 'Family Man'.

The Cult of Domesticity: imposing social order

The Cult of Domesticity is a particular construction of femininity which emphasizes almost exclusively women's alleged nurturant and maternal capacities. These are associated with moral sensibilities by which 'women came to be seen as more morally responsible and of course more chaste than men' (Reiger, 1985: 20). In this construction of femininity, women's lives are structured as dependent and privatized. This is opposed to a masculinity which situates men as actors in the public sphere where they are providers for, and protectors of, women.

The Cult of Domesticity, its practices, and the images of women embedded in it were not indigenous developments. Its themes had been carried from Britain as part of migrants' cultural baggage. Nevertheless, it was not until the latter part of the nineteenth century that conditions developed which allowed the Cult of Domesticity a popular appeal which cut across the boundaries of sex, race, and class, and gave the State a significant interest in its promotion.

The State's interests in the Cult of Domesticity in the 1890s, and its maintenance thereafter, represented a response to threats against the State's own power. The State's very legitimacy rested on the maintenance of public order, but it was increasingly burdened by the victims of social disruption: the elderly, the destitute, and the deserted. The State's fostering of a greater and more rigidly defined domestic role for women embodied a variety of immediate goals. It was an attempt to create a structure of responsibility for the adequate education and control of children. It was undoubtedly oriented towards providing men with incentives to enter family relations which were likely to be economically burdensome. It was also designed to reassert the obligations of individuals to care for their kin and provide a structure through which that care might be facilitated.

Overall, then, women were to be the instruments through which the State could impose domestic order on men and children, and, at the same moment, relieve itself of some of the fiscal burden which accompanied its own intervention into welfare and social reproduction. It is precisely the same intent which underlies the social policy statements regarding such developments as community care in the 1980s. However, while such a reinforcement of the Cult of Domesticity currently draws criticism from feminists, nineteenth century feminists were committed to its establishment.

Feminists of the period were concerned with the exploitation of women's productive labour in the sweated workshops of urban New Zealand and the exploitation of their sexual labour as prostitutes. The Cult of Domesticity inspired and provided a rationale for campaigns to restrict women's access to certain types of paid labour, for the State to define more stringently women's conditions of paid work, and to restrict male's sexual access to women. It also provided the foundation for the demands of feminists to extend rights of citizenship to women.

Women's franchise was pursued not only as an inalienable democratic right consistent with liberal political philosophy; it was also presented as providing women with the legal power to protect their social and economic interests. Moreover, women's alleged moral superiority and conservatism were cited as important reasons for participation in the hitherto corrupt world of male politics (Bunkle, 1980: 66). Women, consequently, were to be the cleaners and purifiers of the private world of the home and of the public world.

Many women involved in the nineteenth century feminist movement came from a burgeoning urban middle class, whose status derived from their training and the sale of their expertise (Reiger, 1985: 34). These women's interest in the Cult of Domesticity reflected not merely their interests as a sex but their class interests. In the late nineteenth and early twentieth centuries, middle-class women were well represented on the boards of hospitals and charitable agencies. A 'woman's sphere' of policy concerns developed, but all women's interests were not necessarily promoted:

They advocated more liberal aid to deserving cases and relatively generous treatment of nursing staff; but high ideals of womanhood and a 'social conscience' might also lead to strong condemnation of persistent offenders, supposedly irresponsible parents, or the second time unmarried mother. (Tennant, 1986: 50.)

Middle-class women and the male professionals, who by the twentieth century had become the prophets of the Cult of Domesticity, associated it with new themes and issues pertinent to an industrial society, and also promised reconciliation between conflicting groups:

... their technical, trained expertise pointed the way to a new social future in which rationally applied knowledge would replace outmoded social conflict. (Reiger, 1985: 22.)

That rationality was to be expressed in the scientific management of the home (Novitz, 1978: 72).

The collapse of a pioneer social order modelled on the social relations of pre-industrial Britain inspired a contrary appeal to the principles of modernity. Communality was replaced with rationality and family. Personal life was to be structured along lines considered compatible with a modern industrial society with women as housewives, the operatives, if not the scientists, of the home. Domestic technology, the routinization of childcare along industrial lines, the standardization of domestic hygiene and diet were initiated by a body of professionals and bureaucrats variously called doctors, home scientists, and child specialists. They extended 'the principles of science and instrumental reason to the operation of the household and to the management of personal relations' (Reiger, 1985: 3).

The elaboration and scientization of housework transformed the role of wife into a profession, albeit an unpaid one. It also contributed to the development of a specifically female sphere in the paid labour market. The Cult of Domesticity, which gave women certain obligations in fulfilling the personal needs of individual men and children (Novitz, 1978: 172), laid the foundation for the feminization of such occupations as teaching and secretarial work. It also stimulated the growth and shape of nursing, domestic science, and other caring professions. These occupations, where women were protected from direct male competition, became increasingly important as a means by which women could achieve some economic independence and social status.

Such developments, together with the legal reforms of the latter part of the nineteenth century, progressively reduced the legal power of fathers and husbands over women's social, economic, and sexual lives. However, the Cult of Domesticity also provided material benefits to men. It may have created a sphere of apparently autonomous female activity but, in fact, it was neither independent of male direction nor did it increase women's overall opportunities within paid labour. The identification of women with the home provided a means by which men could argue for the exclusion of women from the paid labour market. Both women and children had hitherto been employed in factories in preference to men in order to cut costs. Women's and children's wages were lower than men's and as the Sweating Commission uncovered in 1890, they were prepared to work in atrocious conditions.

The Royal Commission on Sweating was set up to inquire into the terms and conditions under which people were employed in New Zealand cities. It was particularly concerned with workers in shops, manufacturing, and hotels. 'Sweating' was defined as working in overcrowded or insanitary conditions, for long and irregular hours, and for low pay. In occupations such as millinery and dressmaking, young girls were frequently expected to work for the first year for nothing. More experienced female workers were often discharged if they asked for wage increases and were replaced by young girls (*Appendix to the Journals of the House of Representatives*, 1890: iv). The conditions related to the Commission by one dressmaker were typical:

. . . I took work home every other night to make up the wages. I found it very trying to my health. . . There is a room underground [in the factory]. It is cold and very damp there. It is cold in the winter and hot in the summer. Some girls left because of the dampness. (*Appendix to the Journal of the House of Representatives*, 1890: 59.)

The Factories Act 1894, and other legislation which arose out of the Sweating Commission, aimed to protect women and children by closely regulating their employment. The advantage to men was that women's and children's labour became less competitive relative to their own.

The Cult of Domesticity asserted men's superiority in spheres of life concerned with ambition, competition, and paid work. It consequently restricted women's participation in those spheres. By the early twentieth century, a male–dominated medical profession used 'scientific' evidence to show that the division of labour between the sexes was biologically determined. In the process, the feminist theme which accompanied the elevation of the roles of wife and mother, that of women's rights to economic independence and access to paid labour, was lost. In 1909, Dr F. C. Batchelor of the Otago Medical School publicly argued that paid labour for women was a:

. . . grave error opposed to the most elementary principles of physiology [and that women studying subjects] for which Nature never intended them. . . [would be victims of] inadequate development of those organs and functions which are characteristic of healthy womanhood. (Olssen, 1980: 167.)

By the early twentieth century, the feminist agenda had been lost from the Cult of Domesticity and those who determined the content of the wife and mother roles were increasingly male professionals. Moreover, the femininity which was being structured through the Cult of

Domesticity was primarily defined in relation to ambiguous notions of masculinity and social problems presented by considerable portions of the male population.

The Man Alone and the Threat to Social Order

Alongside the Cult of Domesticity was a portrayal of masculinity and appropriate male roles. However, while notions of femininity and the roles expected of women found an integrated expression in the Cult of Domesticity, there was no similar unified concept which expressed notions of masculinity and acceptable male roles. There grew up two opposing roles for men, both of which celebrated qualities of strength, reliability, independence, and ambition: the Family Man and the Man Alone.[1] The promotion of the former in association with the Cult of Domesticity was in direct response to the social threat posed by the Man Alone.

Despite the label, the Man Alone did not refer to an isolate, but to a man without a wife. This was a common experience in early colonial New Zealand, imposed by the different ability of British women and men to emigrate. Although men comprised the largest proportion of migrants to the colony, they and the settlement companies were anxious that women too should come to New Zealand. Indeed, assisted immigrant schemes of the mid nineteenth century were specifically designed to ovecome the sex ratio imbalance. About 12,000 young single women, who were brought out to be domestic servants and almost inevitably became wives, arrived on subsidized fares from the mid 1850s to 1871 (Macdonald, 1986: 17). When women did emigrate, the self-sufficient household, in which both reproduction and production were sited, showed a flexible division of labour between the sexes relative to that later developed within the Cult of Domesticity (Graham, 1984: 114-16, 118-26).

Any separation between the sexes, then, derived not from male migrants searching for masculinity in the Antipodes and escaping from the effeminancy of British life (Phillips, 1987: 5), but from the material problem of an imbalance in the sex ratios. In such a context, non-kinship relations with other men formed the basis of men's social existence. Male mateship and self-reliance became the cement of everyday life, both in work and play.

The primary identification of men with men in this early colonial period, unlike later in the nineteenth century, did not, in itself, constitute a gendered culture. Divisions between male- and female-associated roles were too flexible and imprecise in the pioneer context. Furthermore, early colonial life was not apparently marked by any great tension between male mateship on the one hand, and the social relations of mating and kinship on the other. In early colonial New Zealand, the nature of work itself, as well as the frequent siting of production in the household, ensured that men had opportunities to socialize with other men and enabled mateship to be maintained in the workplace itself. The later instrumentalism and efficiency which characterized industrial and urban labour largely destroyed such opportunities. The separation of production from the household forced men to abandon their mates in non-work time as well.

Male mateship and kinship became incompatible because the early colonial household collapsed as a viable unit of support for its members. Prospecting or wage labour became the means of survival and these pursuits required mobility. By the 1860s, it was easier for many men who were looking for paid work to desert their kin than to maintain them. In the gold-fields, the public work-scheme camps, and on the sheep stations, male mateship became an expression of the rejection of kinship and its obligations.

The destitution of women, children, and the elderly reflected the collapse of the early colonial household. It also imposed a significant fiscal burden on the colonial State between the 1860s and 1890s, despite its attempts to eschew responsibility for individuals with kin in the colony (Koopman-Boyden and Scott, 1984: 109-11). Equally important, the obligations and relations embedded in the culture of mateship itself became a threat to social order. Qualities associated with the Man Alone such as independence, egalitarianism, and loyalty became increasingly tied to anti-authoritarianism.

The growth of a mobile male labour force living on casual work was an affront to an already fragile colonial society. It was a threat to the power of the propertied, both rural and urban. Furthermore, anti-authoritarianism, the determination to maintain control over one's own labour, and intra-class loyalty were real barriers to, and inconsistent with, the development of the well-regulated labour force required by industrial capitalists (Fairburn, 1985: 503; Olssen, 1984: 267). The Cult of Domesticity was to be an antidote to this developing sub-culture founded on an elaborate mythology and a conceptualization of masculinity which celebrated the Man Alone. The Cult of Domesticity was used to disarm the challenge of the Man Alone in two ways. Firstly, it provided a basis from which unpropertied men's political power could be countered. Secondly, the Cult of Domesticity was instrumental in defining a less disruptive role for men, as the Family Man. The Cult of Domesticity provided a rhetoric by which women should, by virtue of their purity, be given access to the sphere of politics. The enfranchisement of women in 1893 represented a sometimes uneasy alliance between feminists and propertied men. While feminists saw the vote as a basis for social reform, propertied and powerful men saw women's suffrage as providing them with a new conservative constituency. They believed that women would follow the advice of bourgeois men when it came to vote. Women's suffrage, argued parliamentarian Sir John Hall, would:

> . . . increase the influence of the *settler* [that is, the propertied] and *family-man,* as against the loafing single man who had so great a voice in the last elections. (Cited in Richardson, 1984: 202.)

The promotion of the Cult of Domesticity and the eventual acceptance by propertied and politically active men of women's enfranchisement was prompted by their desire to establish a counterbalance to the disruptive unpropertied male labourers who had been granted the right to vote in 1879.

The creation of a new conservative power in national politics, in the form of the female vote, was of limited use in buttressing the propertied classes against the social disorder of everyday life. Instead, it required a means by which disorderly men could be given a vested interest in a more orderly community.

The Cult of Domesticity implicitly defined the male role as a breadwinner supporting wife and children. It also gave men real benefits. Women's wifely role was transformed from a productive, relatively equal, participant in the early colonial household, to a husband–servicer. However, the promotion of the Cult of Domesticity was, by itself, insufficient. The extent of the desertion and destitution of women and children during the 1880s and 1890s suggests that notions of domesticity were not particularly compelling to men. What was required, then, was a male role which involved the structures implied by the Cult of Domesticity, combined with the attractions associated with the Man Alone. Out of this imperative emerged a masculinity in which the Man Alone was preserved and celebrated, but subordinated to the virtues of the Family Man.

Constructing a New Masculinity: the Family Man

The concept of the Family Man had its foundation in the early colonial household and the mutual dependency of women and men within it. However, men's obligations and responsibilities to kin were transformed in the late nineteenth century into a rigid division of labour in which men's responsibility to women lay in their alleged innate ability to wrest from a hard world, whether rural or urban, a living. Masculinity became increasingly defined in terms of men's responsibilities to their families. This was especially apparent in the campaigns against alcohol in the late nineteenth century:

. . . the disreputable characters who 'loaf around public houses and street corners while their wives and daughters slave to support them' were described as 'devoid of manliness'. On the other hand temperance was presented as a masculine virtue. (Phillips, 1987: 63.)

Thus, the ability to consume alcohol, which was much admired in the Man Alone, became transformed into the Family Man's strength to resist over-indulgence.

Both the Family Man and the Man Alone celebrated qualities of hard work, dependability, pragmatism, self-reliance, and loyalty. But the Family Man had no associations with resistance against men in authority (Phillips, 1987: 40-2). Indeed, the masculinity constructed through the Family Man demanded acceptance of any regulation imposed by involvement in wage labour. It also demanded that men make the privatized family the centre of their everyday lives. Thus, the Family Man came into direct conflict with the Man Alone.

Attracting men into the family required more than the benefits of having an unpaid domestic and sexual servicer in the home, and the co-optation of qualities associated with the Man Alone. It required direct financial incentive. The State's family policy has, since the late nineteenth century, actively redirected income from men and women outside nuclear family structures to men with dependent wives and children. Agricultural settlement and urban housing policies have traditionally favoured married men with dependants, and have been facilitated by the State's accumulation of Māori lands, either through confiscation or appropriation (Brooking, 1984: 226-51; Richardson, 1984: 204-6). Taxation and welfare have similarly been oriented towards supporting the Family Man.

In the private sector, award rates for waged and salaried men have advantaged the married over the single. The youth rate was not merely an expression of differential skills between the young and old, but also reflected assumptions regarding the relative likelihood of supporting dependants. Despite union ambivalence to some of these incentives, they have been maintained by State and employers without great fluctuation for much of the twentieth century.

In essence, then, men were encouraged to assume the burden of supporting women and children because they were able to pursue Family Man and Man Alone constructions of masculinity and gain benefits from both. However, resolution of the seemingly inherent conflict between

the Man Alone, the central motif in relations of mateship, and the Family
Man, crucial to relations of mating, was never completed. Tensions still
exist today. Nevertheless, partial integration was achieved in the
nineteenth century, as it is now maintained, by the institutionalization
of male mateship in certain controlled activities. These activities are
central to male culture.

Male Culture:
reconciling the Man Alone and the Family Man

Male culture in New Zealand successfully incorporates differing styles
and tastes, while being founded on shared activities in both work and
leisure. The focus on activity rather than style allows the differences
between men to be defined as superficial and insignificant and the
apparent differences between men and women to be emphasized.

The major difference between men and women by the late nineteenth
century, as it is today, is the central place of 'work' in men's lives. In
the pioneer period, men's work had been largely manual. The nature
of manual work, which was often co-operative and carried out in isolated
conditions, facilitated male mateship and contributed to the early
construction of masculinity through the Man Alone. While paid work
remained central to masculinity at the end of the nineteenth century,
the nature of work itself had changed. With the development of the
secondary and tertiary sectors of the labour market, fewer men were
involved in manual labour (Brooking 1984: 245; Gardner, 1984: 83).
Moreover, the industrial labour process, which governed relations
between men in the workplace, made the pursuit of affective mateship
relations difficult. The industrial labour process demanded hierarchical,
rather then co-operative work relations, and thus mitigated against
mateship relations being formed between individuals at different levels
of the hierarchy.

Out of these changes emerged two phenomena. Firstly, while manual
work retained its potent association with being 'a man', this was
constructed through the Family Man and within the home rather than
through the Man Alone and in the workplace. By the early twentieth
century, manual labour was becoming the basis of a strict division of
labour in the household (Toynbee, 1984). This is still widespread today.
Men predominate in doing renovations in and around the home, in
caring for the vegetable garden (in keeping with their role as provider),
and in car and equipment maintenance (Fletcher, 1978; Gray, 1983; James
1985). 'Do-it-yourself' activity echoes the self-sufficiency of the pioneer,
but it is not necessarily connected with male mateship. Instead, it is often

carried out alone and is a major part of a man's identification with the family. As one Kawerau woman said of her husband:

He does his bit ... all that roofing, fencing, driveway, fixes our car and any appliances that break. He potters around the home an awful lot. (James, 1985: 161.)

Secondly, changes in production meant that although workmates remained a primary reference group for men, the significance of work lay in the affinity it gave men who shared the responsibilities of being family breadwinners. Under these conditions, the creation and maintenance of mateship relations were transferred from the place of work to the sites of leisure. Sports, pubs, and service clubs provided the context of mateship while at the same time confining those activities so they did not pose a threat to men's obligations and responsibilities as the Family Man.

Sports and service clubs were, and remain, venues in which male mateship could be expressed without posing a threat to social order. Increasingly formalized during the late nineteenth and early twentieth centuries, sports, particularly rugby, not only provided an outlet for the aggressive tendencies celebrated as a male virtue, but also a context in which intimate contact could be maintained between men (Phillips, 1987: 86–130). Moreover, it was a contact controlled and directed by professional and propertied men (de Jong, 1987: 48).

Male mateship may have constituted a threat to the professional and propertied classes in the 1880s, but by the twentieth century, rugby had contributed to mateship becoming a pillar of the social order. Certainly, conflict between the rugby hierarchy of officials and the players was not uncommon. Nevertheless, this was controlled and identified, not as anti-authoritarianism or expressions of class styles in conflict, but as conflict between player and non-player, young and old. Above all, rugby (and undoubtedly other sports) fostered strong feelings of community, kinship, and egalitarianism among men of differing social and economic positions (de Jong, 1987: 49–50).

Rugby was not a threat to the Family Man. It created the 'character' necessary to youths who would inevitably become providers for women. It also had its own sunset clause. Age ensured that the joys of mateship centred on the rugby field would eventually be transformed into the joys of family. More importantly, such a transformation could be achieved without involving men in a rejection of mateship itself. Absorption into domesticity was presented not as a betrayal of male loyalties but as part of the process of ageing.

Even today, rugby allows the integration of the Family Man and the Man Alone. The family waits on the sidelines; parents, siblings, and girlfriends are relied on as spectators (de Jong, 1987: 41). And female relatives have always been expected to perform domestic chores for the club and its players. Women's support of men's sports is so much taken for granted that to question it can become a political strategy. During the proposed All Black rugby tour to South Africa in 1985, the group, Women Against Rugby (WAR), urged women to express their political protest by refusing to wash rugby jerseys (Smith, 1985).

The most ambiguous site of male mateship activity has been the pub. In the late nineteenth century, the promotion of the Cult of Domesticity by feminists had at the same moment been an all-out attack on alcohol consumption by men (Bunkle, 1980: 52-76). Indeed, the Women's Christian Temperance Union provided the vehicle for New Zealand's most vociferous suffragettes. For them, alcohol was associated with male drunkenness and disorder, and the cause of desertion, destitution, and physical attacks against women. Liquor was served in the same houses as women were offered as prostitutes, and thus alcohol became linked to the spread of venereal disease (Eldred-Grigg, 1984: 32). Despite this, the liquor lobby was too strong, and the place of alcohol in colonial life too deeply embedded, for prohibition to occur. Consequently, the pub remained a place of virtually unrestrained male conviviality, from which women were excluded. This exclusion was a custom which did not need to be supported by legislation, although the 1922 Hockley Committee on licensing suggested that women be legally prohibited from public bars (Phillips, 1987: 76). The pub, then, was an arena in which the tensions in male culture between the Family Man and the Man Alone emerged.

The introduction of six o'clock closing in 1920 merely defined the line between public and private, mateship and mating, work and intimate life more rigidly, and exacerbated the oppositions within men's lives. In the 'six o'clock swill', which rapidly became ritualized, men retreated to the pub for a precious hour or so before being privatized in the home. Opening hours provided a retreat both from work and wife (Phillips, 1987: 75-80). The abolition of six o'clock closing in 1967 did little to undermine the male exclusivity of the pub. It is hardly surprising that some of the first feminist actions during the 1970s involved the invasion of public bars. Even in the early 1980s, some public bars in Auckland and Wellington refused entrance to women (Dann, 1985: 6).

Tensions in Pākehā Gendered Culture

The resolution for men of the conflict between the Family Man and the Man Alone was expressed in the creation of a set of activities which were exclusive of women. The most women could expect was that men should support them economically, preferably not beat them, and, again preferably, not commit adultery. If men did beat their wives or commit adultery, there was very little women could legally do about it. Men could pursue the activities of mateship knowing that they could, when the benefits of conviviality had worn thin, be revived and sometimes repaired in the home. The role of the Family Man, while demanding that men shoulder the burden of the economic support of women and children, required little intense interaction with them. Consequently, the Cult of Domesticity was progressively transformed into a mere adjunct of masculinity.

By the early twentieth century, the Cult of Domesticity was not only promoted and defined by male professionals who had removed any vestiges of its initial feminist agenda, but female culture had become the facilitator of male culture. Some women may have privately denigrated men's mateship activities, but the wife's role in the home was extended to supporting those activities. Provincial shows, race meetings, and rugby matches all depended on the mobilization of wives' domestic skills.

The very dependency of mateship activities and masculinity on women's co-operation makes it in the interests of men to intervene in, and to take control of, women's activities. Such dependence also presents a threat to men's assumed independence and authority. It is these contradictions which underlie the gendered culture in New Zealand.

The emergence of future social problems out of the contradictions embedded in a gendered culture, did not concern those who promoted new notions of femininity and masculinity in the late nineteenth and early twentieth centuries. Their immediate desire was to reconstruct a social order torn apart by structural conflicts. It was not only the relations between men and women, but also those of propertied and unpropertied, and Māori and Pākehā, which were to be resolved through this gendered culture.

The construction of masculinity which integrated the Man Alone and the Family Man incorporated all men irrespective of race or class. The inclusiveness of male culture was a direct consequence of its development as a mechanism by which potentially disruptive social groups of men might be co-opted and controlled. Similarly, the Cult of Domesticity provided a rationale for intervention into the lives of the working class and, later the Māori. Indeed, the Cult of Domesticity, which the State had so assiduously promoted for the Pākehā, became an important means by which the Māori could be assimilated into Pākehā society.

Māori Assimilation into the Gendered Culture

The desire to assimilate the Māori emerged from two quite disparate developments. Firstly, by the twentieth century, it became clear that the Māori population would not, as expected after the Anglo-Māori Wars, decline to virtual extinction. Once again, this raised for the Pākehā the issue of the relationship of Māori to Pākehā society. Secondly, eugenic policies directed towards the expansion of the British 'race'[2] were becoming popular in New Zealand as in other western societies.

According to many in New Zealand, the problem of social order related not simply to the control of the morally and physically weak: the indigent, the poor, and the criminal. There was also the problem of racial degradation by 'enemies' outside society. The British 'race' was believed to be under threat from other 'races'. However, the Māori as a 'race' was not the target of eugenicist rhetoric. Perhaps Pākehā viewed the Māori, relegated as they were to the margins of society, as numerically and economically unthreatening. Perhaps it reflected a certain ambivalence in Pākehā attitudes to the Māori. The Māori was initially the 'noble savage' and latterly the comical 'Hori' (McGeorge, 1981: 20). Neither image posed a threat to the dominance of the white 'races'. It was the Asian who was regarded as the real polluter of the 'race'.

This was clearly evident in discussions preceding the Immigration Restriction Act 1920, which represented a State commitment to eugenics and its acceptance of popularly expressed abhorrence at the possibility of a 'piebald New Zealand' (O'Connor, 1968: 53). Despite crude references to colour, however, this was not a matter of mere colour discrimination. Asians were regarded as a threat to Māori racial purity too. An Auckland group, the Akarana Association which was founded by both Māori and Pākehā, publicly expressed opposition to Asian and Māori inter-marriage. The alleged vulnerability of Māori women to so-called predatory Asian males inspired the National Council of Women to declare that: 'Europeans are bound in every way to assist the Māoris in overcoming the Asiatic evil' (Leckie, 1985: 126). This proposed alliance against the Asians recalls the myth of the Aryan Māori promulgated by Tregear, in which the Māori was regarded not as an inferior race 'but a wayward younger brother who could be saved' (Belich, 1986: 300) through assimilation. The imposition of the Cult of Domesticity was part of this salvation.

The concern of eugenics groups for the purity of the white 'race', and the movement for the scientization of housework, expressed important common themes. Most notably these included a concern with reproductive fitness, the regulation of child-rearing, the control of sexuality, the maintenance of social order, an understanding of society as essentially biologically determined, and a commitment to social engineering through modern scientific practice (Eldred–Grigg, 1984: 125). All these relied on an understanding of women's role as domestic, nurturant, and being socially responsible.

Home management was promoted by both the Government and Māori professionals as the means to achieve a healthy Māori population. Maui Pomare, a prominent doctor who became the first Māori Health Officer in 1900 and an MP in 1912, was instrumental in bringing health services to Māori communities. Furthermore, despite the Native School system, Māori and Pākehā school children were exposed to similar educational experiences which reinforced gender roles. Māori girls were prepared for adult roles as wives and mothers, and Māori boys, like their Pākehā counterparts, were given agricultural, manual, and other vocational training (King, 1984: 283).

After the Second World War, the imposition of this gendered culture on the Māori was associated with the Māori Women's Welfare League. The League explicitly advocated the preservation and promotion of Māori culture, but it was also involved in disseminating Pākehā skills in homecraft and mothercraft among Māori women. In particular, it focused on equipping Māori mothers with the skills to cope and be accepted by Pākehā as competent members of an advanced industrial society. For the League, the adoption of Pākehā techniques of domestic labour was symbolic of Māori equality with Pākehā. Domesticity was more than an occupation, it reflected a moral status.

It was for this reason that the Māori Women's Welfare League, the New Zealand Māori Council, and other Māori and Pākehā leaders made a vociferous attack on the primary school journal, *Washday at the Pa,* in 1964. The League particularly objected to the way in which the journal depicted, through the photographs of Ans Westra, a Māori family living in an economically depressed rural area (Walsh, 1964). Arguing that the journal portrayed a negative image of Māori society, because it recorded substandard housing and a lack of basic household amenities, the League successfully demanded that the journal be withdrawn. This not only illustrated Māori sensitivity to Pākehā judgements, but the overriding dominance of technological and scientific rationality in determining what was, or was not, competent housekeeping and childcare. As one newspaper commented, there had developed in both Pākehā and Māori society a 'confusion of good home management with the machines which can be used to achieve it' (cited in Walsh, 1964: 342).

Winiata (1967: 119) suggests that the League's promotion of home and mothercrafts expressed a commitment to the amenities associated with the nuclear family rather than with traditional Māori family structures. This provided a basis for the strong relationship between the League and successive Governments. Both assumed that the nuclear family and women's role within it had a moral significance. Māori women, like their Pākehā counterparts, became regarded as the nurturers of the next generation. Māori women were presented as the moral force which would solve problems experienced by the Māori, from substandard housing to poor health. Many League members embraced the philosophy that 'the root causes of Maori problems were centred around the mother, the child and the home' (Szaszy, 1973).

Although Pākehā efforts to assimilate the Māori and the Cult of Domesticity came together in many policies directed towards or imposed on the Māori, the Māori response was not a passive one. Like Pākehā women, who have derived benefits from the establishment of the Cult of Domesticity, Māori women too exploited the possibilities provided by Pākehā policies for self-determination. Thus, through their League membership, many Māori women took up one of the few political avenues available to them in their quest to preserve their culture and solve the problems which arose from the structure of inequalities of race in New Zealand.

The Gendered Culture: creating order or disorder in the 1980s?

The gendered culture, which pervades New Zealand life and cultural expression, hinges on a masculinity structured through the Family Man and the Man Alone, and on a femininity structured through the Cult of Domesticity. The development of these material and ideological structures derived directly from a crisis in social order in which the structures of race, class, and sex relations had been disrupted and were in overt conflict.

For much of the twentieth century, the gendered culture has allowed social order to be maintained. In most societies, certainly in New Zealand, lack of disorder is gladly accepted as indicative of an absence of conflict. But, in fact, the oppositions which initially gave rise to the gendered culture, although transformed in detail, still exist. Māori and Pākehā, the unpropertied and the propertied, women and men were in real material conflict and those conflicts of interest re-emerged in new ways in the 1970s and 1980s. This is evidenced in the land marches, the feminist movement, and protests against playing rugby with South Africa. For many, the alleged disorders of the 1980s — criminality, violence, pornography, industrial unrest, alcohol and drug addiction, economic uncertainty, and racial conflict — are all expressions of a collapse in the division of labour between the sexes which is central to the gendered culture. Underlying this is a usually covert, although sometimes explicit, mythology in which social disorder is connected with sins against nature. Even Jock Phillips starts his detailed critical study of images of Pākehā masculinity in New Zealand with reference to socio-biological differences between men and women. In his fallacious[3] summary of the division of labour in pre-Victorian Britain, he argues:

While the men walked out to toil in the fields, the women, perhaps because of their child-rearing function were more likely to be found around the home . . . Men also tended to carry out those jobs demanding great physical strength. (Phillips, 1987: 5.)

Furthermore, Phillips assumes that it was British men's separation from the allegedly traditional conflict with nature which motivated them to seek a life in the colonies. Thus, masculine culture in New Zealand, even among its most ardent critics, is ultimately associated with natural predispositions.

If nature and order are inherently associated, the key to the reconstruction of New Zealand society today, as it was in the nineteenth century, lies in a reinforcement of the Cult of Domesticity and women's dependency on men. *However, the gendered culture is not natural.* It is a social development deriving from the particular exigencies of British colonialism in Aotearoa. Furthermore, the gendered culture itself is progressively being acknowledged, and not only by feminists, as a source of social disorder and social problems. Male culture is once again becoming a threat to social order, but so too is female culture.

1 We use the terms 'Family Man' and 'Man Alone' to denote two contrasting ideals of the male role. These terms derive from a growing literature which explores the characteristics of masculinity (for overseas examples, see David and Brannon, 1976; Tolson, 1977; and for a New Zealand account, see Phillips, 1987). Our discussion is not simply concerned with elaborating the various images and dimensions of the male sex role, but with developing an analysis of the historical development of the *structure* of masculinity in our society.

2 At this time it was commonly believed that populations formed distinct racial groups. The concept of race which the eugenicists pursued was based on invalid pseudo-scientific evidence and a confusion between physical, social, and cultural attributes. (For further elaboration on 'race', see Spoonley, 1988.)

3 Although there was a tendency for agricultural work in the eighteenth century to be increasingly divided according to sex, in pre-industrial Britain men and women generally did similar work. Pahl (1984: 20-5) summarizes much of the research which indicates that both women and men toiled in the fields. Women used horse-drawn harrows and undertook a variety of jobs including haymaking, weeding, mowing, and driving plough oxen. Unmarried and widowed men looked to marry or remarry quickly, not only because of women's contribution to around-the-house work, but also because there were more people to work the land (Chaytor, 1980: 38).

The Contemporary Practice of Masculinity and Femininity

There is a commonly expressed belief in this society that New Zealanders excel more overseas than at home. Some have suggested that this reflects the negative impact of hitherto stringent regulation of our social and economic life by the State (James, 1986: 14-15). This is hardly convincing. In the mid-eighties deregulation has been associated with continued migration overseas, high international profiles among our large companies, and, of course, among our sports people, while at home the problems of violence, poverty, and the wastage of human resources through drug abuse and road deaths has continued unabated.

The problems of waste and disorder in New Zealand society are deeply profound, and State regulation is merely a response rather than a cause of it. If New Zealand society is restrictive of the 'human spirit', if it is violent and suppressed (McLaughlan, 1976), these tendencies lie not in the Welfare State but in a much longer history. It lies in the particular construction of masculinity and femininity found in this country.

We are loath to admit this. Our gendered culture appears so natural to us that it is rarely considered at all systematically. Repeatedly, various committees, starting with the 1979 Select Committee on Violent Offending and culminating in the Ministerial Committee of Inquiry into Violence (1987), have tackled the problem of disorder. None has engaged with the problems created by the particular construction of masculinity and femininity in New Zealand. The problem of gender and its relation to social disorder is reduced to superficial assertions regarding the negative portrayal of women by the media and the celebration by that same media of machismo (Ministerial Committee, 1987: 15, 55, 57).

The images associated with masculinity and femininity are not the source of problems in New Zealand. Instead it is the very organization of male and female cultures. It is the dynamics of each of these cultures, together and apart, which underpin many of the immediate and obvious social problems with which our society is presently confronted. In order to understand these social problems, we must consider the structure and processes which constitute the gendered culture today.

The Structure of Male Culture

In contemporary male culture the motifs of the Family Man and the Man Alone still remain very strong. These are more than ideas or archetypes. They represent significant structures around which masculinity is established and continued. The male way of life, male culture, involves being primarily associated with paid labour. The vast majority of adult men are involved in the labour market, either as employees or employers.

According to the 1981 census, only 22 per cent of men over fifteen years of age are outside the full-time labour force. Compare this to almost 61 per cent of women (Department of Statistics, 1987: 358-9). Despite the progressive movement of married and single women into paid labour, men still tend to be the major breadwinners in the households they share with women. They are, in fact, family men. Even when they fail to provide adequately for dependent women and children, they remain for many women their only channel of access to the cash economy (Novitz, 1987b; Saville-Smith, 1987a: 198). Male culture is shaped within the context of this economic independence. It is shaped also by geographical mobility.

To get to the workplace, men must leave their homes. Associated with this is the opportunity to construct social networks outside the familial household. These social relations are independent of and seldom governed by those existing within the home. Consequently, while men popularly describe their familial breadwinner role as entrapping, in reality it actually breaks down the boundaries and constraints imposed by obligations to kin and family. It is women, rather than men, who most carefully maintain relations between family members and the wider kin group (Stivens, 1978).

Although the Family Man is central to the male culture, men are largely absentee parents and husbands (Donnelly, 1978: 92). Obligations to wives and children are primarily financial (James, 1987: 111; Novitz, 1987b: 37) and while more men seem to be having more contact with their children, this still tends to be either as disciplinarians or in play (Ritchie and Ritchie, 1978: 19). Research suggests that women's expectations of husbands are similarly restricted to their fulfilment of financial obligations and jobs such as home decoration, repairs, and outside work. Such tasks occupy relatively little time compared to daily household tasks, and tend to be irregular rather than regular commitments (Novitz, 1987b: 45-8).

The structural context of male culture encourages the formation of social relations outside family and kin networks rather than within them. Consequently, women have a peculiarly tangential position *vis-á-vis* men's world. Masculinity, almost by definition, is informed by the dynamics of mateship rather than by the dynamics associated with mating.

Although men's involvement in paid work is central to male culture, the mateship which is integral to male culture cannot be pursued within the workplace itself. The hierarchical organization of paid work conflicts with the particular combination of individualism and egalitarianism which marks mateship relations. These must be established outside the place of work, even if the participants in those relations are in fact colleagues. Equally, mateship tends to be pursued outside the home even among male kin. The sites of male conviviality have remained virtually unchanged over the last century. They are to be found in the sports clubs, the playing fields, the businessmen's and working men's clubs, and the pubs. These are the places where men can call because of the mobility conferred on them by their paid labour outside, and their limited responsibilities within, the home.

The Practices of Male Mateship

Within the sites of male conviviality, mateship consists of a celebration and reaffirmation of masculinity. Central to this is an assertion of the abstract symbols of masculinity, particularly sexual/physical power, self control, and control over others. This is often achieved through ritual behaviour.[1] For instance, in public places men's sexual overtures to women unknown to them are primarily attempts to impress male associates with their sexual mastery and, equally important, fearlessness. The risk for men who publicly proposition women is humiliation. This element of risk repeats itself in many of the ritualized forms of male mateship behaviour. These range from the often savage initiation rites in boys' schools and university hostels, to the antics of the Red Squad preparing themselves to confront protestors during the Springbok Tour.

The risk associated with violence is central to many of men's leisure activities. Mataira (1987) notes that violence ritualized in the game 'argy-bargy' is an important means by which men gain status within, and prove allegiance to, their mateship group. Played mainly by rugby-club members in a small North Island East Coast community, 'argy-bargy' consists of knocking group members to the ground:

Once on the ground one had to fight back to regain status among the group. . . to disguise all the brutality, laughing and joking was always a large part of the group's activity. . . Argy-bargy was considered by some group members to be a 'sociable' act because it was something they expressed themselves and something they all shared in common. (Mataira, 1987: 129, 131.)

Risk also underlies alcohol's central place in male culture. The use of alcohol strengthens the bonds of male mateship by delimiting the boundaries between masculine and feminine worlds. It is also a means by which individual men assert their manhood relative to each other. Alcohol is a key ingredient in male socializing, recreation, and ritual precisely because it carries the risk that the imbiber will lose his virility, his physical power, and his control (Hodges, 1985). Alcohol consumption is a sport in which demonstrating drinking prowess is simultaneously a demonstration of power.

Drinking culture is definitively and exclusively a male domain. Not only are men less likely than women to be non-drinkers, the majority of heavy drinkers are men (Caswell, 1980: 2-4). Indeed, the differences between the nature of male and female drinking are so marked that while the overall alcohol consumption of women has increased in recent years, with the exception of drink-driving incidents, women have not yet displayed any increase in alcohol-related rates of mortality or morbidity (Park, 1985: 80).

Of men, young men from eighteen to twenty-three years are most likely to drink large amounts of alcohol (Casswell, 1980: 3). This is directly related to their search for entry into the institution of mateship. Alcohol consumption is part of the rites of passage into manhood. This explains the involvement of young men in the most ritualized form of drinking behaviour, drinking games. In the course of his fieldwork studying male drinking styles in Dunedin, Hodges (1985) discovered an array of drinking games: Alcohol Bonging, Hokonui Swindle, Matches, Bottles, Fluffy Ducks, Bunnies are Hovering, Cardinal Huff, Psych, All Blacks, The Amazing Grimaldi Brothers, and High Candelabras. Some demanded that individuals display physical or mental control to *avoid* drinking to excess. Others demanded that control be maintained *despite* drinking to excess. Hodges (1985: 13-14) describes in some detail the traditional drinking game in one male college of Otago University. Apart from the consumption of six bottles of Speights Ale in four hours, its purpose was clearly to divide the 'men' from the boys. Those who succeeded: '. . . were Men, resolutely with a capital M, while [those who failed] were "chunder bunnies" or "coma kids" ' (Hodges, 1985: 14).

Given the frequent connection between alcohol consumption and attempts to demonstrate control, it is hardly surprising that many men insist on driving after drinking.[2] Again, risk is a central element in this activity. Drinking and driving is encouraged by the association of mechanical things with the male world of production. For working-class men and men of other low status groups, their access to alcohol and vehicles is one of the means of gaining limited status and one of their few sites of autonomy. Connell (1983: 29) eloquently identifies the struggles of young working-class men to achieve acceptance in an adult and bourgeois-dominated culture:

The points on which the issue of control is fought out, smoking, drinking, driving, fucking, foul language and physical aggression, are an inextricable mixture of claims to adulthood and claims to masculinity. Their barrenness reflects the very limited claims that can be made by people who, because of the age and class structure, have very few resources.

Drinking and driving is, essentially, a male ritual. That is, it is a form of behaviour with clear meaning to both the individual and his peers.

Ritualized mateship behaviour is also found on the sports field, particularly the rugby field. Rugby combines both the socially valued aspects of male culture and its more anti-social elements. Phillips (1987: 86) describes it as bringing together 'two powerful traditions: the desire to keep alive the muscular virtues of a pioneering heritage, and the concern to contain that masculine spirit within respectable boundaries'. Rugby is credited with building fine minds and bodies and fostering team spirit and a sense of solidarity. But, from its earliest days, rugby has also been associated with drinking and the pub (Phillips, 1987: 94). The unofficial legend of the hard-drinking, hard-playing All Blacks, notes Phillips (1987: 125-7), includes boozey orgies and violence to property and individuals both on and off the field. Drinking games and rough play are just as much part of rugby as leadership and skill.

Male Culture as National Identity

Perhaps because rugby so neatly integrates the disparate elements of male culture (the group dependency, the risk, the violence, and the virility), the game has been the means by which the images embedded in male culture have become synonymous with the national character. It was not simply the sacrifices made in the Boer and Great Wars but the first international rugby tours in the late nineteenth and early twentieth centuries which inspired and coalesced national sentiment (Sinclair, 1986: 13). The association of rugby with heroism and prestige has been so strong that it has made many a non-sporting boy's life a misery. Ability on the rugby field is a ready-made road to success that no other sporting codes (nor most occupations) provide. As one of *The Jones Men* (a group of men studied by Gray, all with the surname Jones) said:

I played rugby right through school. . . If you weren't in the first fifteen and you took a technical course you were nobody. If you were in the First Fifteen and needed help with anything, that was it, you got it. If you were rugby you were everything. (Gray, 1983: 30.)

It is this conflation between masculinity, rugby, and national identity which has made the debates over rugby links with South Africa so vociferous. The conflicts over the 1981 Springbok Tour exposed deep rifts within New Zealand society. The debate over the tour was about sport and international politics, racism, and, according to one commentator, sexism.

What gets done through rugby *is* politics, not in the first place the politics of racism, but the politics of sex. Rugby is and has been about the organisation of actual and symbolic relationships among men and, by indirection, the disorganisation of relationships among women. (Fougere, 1981: 2.)

In fact, the tour did confront issues of inequality of race, but it did so through the prism of a gendered culture.

In the past, rugby had successfully fostered camaraderie among men from diverse ethnic, or social backgrounds. For Māori men in particular, the 1981 tour threw up profound personal conflicts. Their involvement as Māori in anti-racist protests threatened the benefits of mateship and social status they gained from playing rugby with Pākehā men. As Ripeka Evans pointed out at the time:

Maori men have more to lose over the Tour because of the sexist connection with rugby. For Maori men, rugby has been a bargaining ground. (Cited in Coney, 1981: 1.)

Dann (1982: 27), too, noted that working-class men, both Māori and Pākehā, tended to support rugby:

. . . for all the reasons most middle class men no longer need it — for recreation (instead of the arts or more individualistic sports), for masculine identity (in a homophobic culture), and for national identity of a sort they can readily understand, approve of and even achieve personally.

By contrast, neither Māori nor Pākehā women had these conflicts of interest and were prominent in anti-tour action.

Māori women were particularly evident in leadership positions in protests against the tour. But for all women, the tour allowed them to express their hostility to male practices and values:

. . . although it was the done thing to aver that one was opposed to racism, not rugby, I suspect that if many of the female anti-tourists were to come clean they would admit it was six of one and half a dozen of the other. . . many women were happy to express a public disdain for the game which they had previously had to keep quiet. (Dann, 1982: 27-8.)

Phillips (1987: 262) argues that for some men also the tour provided a context in which traditional male culture could be questioned:

On 18 August 1956 I marched off to a rugby ground to watch my heroes battle with the Springboks... On 18 August 1981, exactly 25 years later, I again marched off to a rugby ground... this time I was marching off to a rugby ground, not to cheer on my heroes, but to protest against the playing of the game to stop people watching it. For myself as for the thousands of others who marched in protest the primary focus was a disgust that New Zealand should host representatives of a regime built upon racism. Yet the protest also represented a challenge to the male stereotype. Rugby contests with South Africa had traditionally been peacetime's sternest tests of the nation's virility.

1981 may have been a catastrophic year for rugby and even for male culture, but traditional masculine images still symbolize our national identity. New Zealand's America's Cup Challenge in 1986 not only presented a new sporting quest for the kiwi male, but also new ways of asserting masculinity through a combination of sporting and business success. Gooding's 'inside story' of the Cup Challenge (itself a celebration of male culture) demonstrated the way business has become the new frontier in which men can prove their manhood:

Michael Fay has managed another coup. Not only has he auctioned seven America's cup replicas for more than a *hundred grand apiece*; he's also inspired other dinner guests to donate such diverse goodies as sections and stallion services to the campaign. STALLION SERVICES! The ultimate macho thing for any businessman to donate. I hereby give you SEMEN! (Gooding, 1987: 37.)

However, if sponsors present yachting as indisputably masculine, it also needs the support of female New Zealand. Just as women could not hope to sacrifice all for their country during the wars but they could keep the 'home fires burning', so challenges for the Admiral's and America's Cups could not go on without women's services and women's sacrifices.

As much planning seems to go into the yachties' menus as into the race itself. Women running a household know the continual responsibility of planning and preparing meals, but consider producing nutritionally balanced food for the Admiral's Cup team of forty. One of the two female cooks enthused, 'It's good Kiwi girls cooking good Kiwi food for Kiwi blokes' (Coughlan, 1987: 14). Typically, this behind the scenes work went largely unacknowledged by the tough silent yachties — ' "Good chomp, girls" is top praise' (Coughlan, 1987: 17). Thus, female culture, while excluded from the symbols of national identity, is demanded for the national effort.

Female Culture: structured dependency

Within New Zealand's gendered culture, female culture is relegated to supporting the 'male way of life'. However, this is not to say that female culture is a mere derivative of male culture. Nor can the costs associated with a gendered culture be reduced to a construction of masculinity in New Zealand. Even those costs which fall most heavily on women, such as male sexual and domestic violence, dependency, and sheer impoverishment, cannot be adequately explained by reference to the dynamics of male culture alone. The gendered culture in New Zealand consists of more than merely male cultural practices; it also incorporates a strong female culture constituted through the Cult of Domesticity. This is a culture women actively create and maintain, just as men maintain male culture. Despite its costs, and despite the critiques of it by feminists, many women remain outspokenly committed to it.

Like male culture, female culture represents a compound of essentially contradictory images and organizational forms. Just as masculinity embodies often conflicting motifs of the Family Man and the Man Alone, femininity is structured around the Dependent Woman and the Moral Redemptress. The contradiction is clear. While women's dependence underpins their real subordination to and exploitation by men, the motif of woman as Moral Redemptress portrays women as powerful beings able to save men, and indeed society, from male anarchic tendencies.

The organizational features of female culture have been remarked upon at length in feminist literature (see James, 1987; Novitz, 1987b; Saville-Smith 1987a). Women are primarily identified with and committed to work they carry out, unpaid, within the home. That work consists of both the fulfilment of partner's and children's material needs through housework, and their psychological needs through emotional support. The primacy of this commitment remains whether or not women are within paid labour. Women may work in both the home and in the paid labour force, but it is the former work which defines females in our society as 'women'.

Women's culture is governed by the shape of the private sphere. The private sphere itself is determined by the requirements of a male culture situated in the public sphere of paid work (James, 1987; Novitz, 1987b). More importantly, the private sphere is relegated by the very nature of our cash-economy to a position of functional dependence on the public. For women, this implies not so much exclusion from the public sphere (at no time have women as a group been entirely absent from paid labour), but that they, as the dominant actor in the private sphere, ultimately become dependent on the dominant actor in the public sphere (men).

It is the nature of this dependency which distinguishes the contemporary shape of the Cult of Domesticity from that promoted in the late nineteenth century. The latter was developed with a strong emphasis on the exchange between men and women of economic support for skills in domestic production such as preserving fruit, baking, bread-making, sewing, needlework, soap-making, and the care of domestic livestock such as poultry. Since the Second World War, however, the need for domestic production of this type has diminished. Most of the goods consumed in the home are now produced in the manufacturing sector. Many of the services, such as nursing and hygiene, which wives were trained to provide, have been taken over by health and welfare professionals. Under these circumstances, domestic work has become de-skilled. Associated with this, the housewife has experienced a loss of status, despite the fact that she still works long hours within the home.

The problem for women is twofold. Firstly, the most obvious services they now provide, such as cleaning and cooking, are not popularly regarded as work, let alone skilled work, which should attract social rewards. Secondly, the emotional, psychological, and sexual services they provide, which on the paid labour market would be considered skilled and consequently highly paid, cannot be accounted for in the home in the same way as traditional domestic production. The invisibility of women's skilled work within the home is exacerbated by the fact that women are not trained explicitly to undertake such services in the same way that in the past women were trained in the skills of domestic production and childcare in domestic science courses and organizations such as the Plunket Society. Consequently, while women's work in the home is both real and often skilled, the relations between men and women are increasingly marked by female dependency, rather than material exchanges to their mutual benefit.

Female culture is not simply an aggregation of tasks undertaken in the home (many of those tasks, women undertake in paid labour in any case), it is a culture of economic dependency. It is also a culture of poverty. Indeed, impoverishment is the most clear, if most frequently ignored, feature of women's dependency (Table 1).

In 1986 almost 60 per cent of adult women had incomes of $10,000 or less in comparison to only 29.3 per cent of adult men (Horsfield, 1988: 338). Almost 30 per cent of all women, single and married, appeared to have no incomes at all in 1981 (Department of Statistics, 1987: 357-9). In the years 1984-1985, 46 per cent of married women had no incomes derived from paid labour (Hall, 1987: 19). They, like many women, were probably reduced to a personal income provided by the State through the family benefit.

This does not, of course, imply that these women's standard of living reflects their real exclusion from income and wealth. The majority of women have a standard of living far in excess of that which would be

Table 1: Income of Persons Aged Fifteen Years and Over, by Sex, 1986 Census

Income group ($)	Male (%)	Female (%)
2,500 or less	7.4 (27.3)*	18.9 (72.7)*
2,501 - 5,000	3.2 (27.9)	7.9 (72.1)
5,001 - 7,500	10.5 (34.4)	19.2 (65.6)
7,501 - 10,000	8.2 (36.9)	13.6 (63.1)
10,001 - 15,000	18.5 (51.2)	17.0 (48.8)
15,001 - 20,000	17.3 (63.8)	9.4 (36.2)
20,001 - 25,000	12.8 (75.0)	4.1 (25.0)
25,001 - 30,000	8.2 (83.4)	1.6 (16.6)
30,001 - 40,000	6.4 (88.5)	0.8 (11.5)
40,001 and over	3.9 (91.0)	0.4 (9.0)
Not specified	3.7 (33.2)	7.2 (66.8)

* Figures in parentheses refer to the percentage of each income group that are male or female.
Source: Based on Horsfield, 1988: 338.

available to them by virtue of their own incomes or control over property. This is because of the exchanges between men and women within households. Nevertheless, it does mean that many women who break the economic bonds they have with their partners must confront the reality of their own, and frequently their children's, potential impoverishment. The experience of this Kawerau woman is, in many ways, typical. The fear of impoverishment undoubtedly kept her in marriage:

I don't think I'd be able to survive as a solo parent. . . our lifestyle would change dramatically. We couldn't afford to live the way we do. You know, its the fact you have to go out and find somewhere else to live. Pulling the kids out of school, because I couldn't stay here, I could never live it down. . . I would have to leave. Why should I leave a two storey home to him?[3]

The impoverishment of women cannot be solved by entry into wage labour.

Even women who have independently earned incomes are restricted in their earning power. Because women spend so much less time in paid labour, they are unlikely to accumulate wealth (Novitz, 1987b: 33-4). In 1981, a fifteen-year-old male entering paid labour could expect to have a paid working life of almost forty-six years. A female of the same age could expect a paid working life of less than twenty years (Department of Statistics, 1987: 354). Under these conditions it is hardly surprising that women's wealth, as represented by the value of their estates, is only around 79 per cent of men's (Saville-Smith, 1987a: 198). Women's earning power is also adversely affected by their over-representation in the part-time labour force (Novitz, 1987b: 33). Women earn less than men because they are often excluded from penal rates associated with overtime. They also tend to become established in a secondary labour market in which there are few career opportunities, little job security, and low remuneration. Nursing, clerical and sales work, food processing, and clothing manufacture are all structured around the secondary labour market. They are occupational sectors which are relatively poorly paid to the extent that, despite the 1972 Equal Pay Act, women's hourly rates of pay in 1987 were still less than 80 per cent of men's hourly rates and their average total weekly earnings were only 72.2 per cent of men's weekly earnings (Horsfield, 1988: 325).

Māori women as a group are particularly vulnerable to impoverishment. In 1981, their median income was only 80 per cent of that for non-Māori women. Of all men and women, they are the group most likely to receive no income at all, and least likely to have an income over $20,000 (Horsfield and Evans, 1988: 66).

Limited opportunities in paid labour are directly connected to women's association with the home. The service and caring occupations into which women are channelled on the labour market mirror the tasks they undertake at home. The tendency for those occupations to be rewarded at considerably lower rates reflects not so much a belief that such occupations are without value, but rather that women gain intrinsic rewards in doing them. In addition, it is frequently assumed that the skills used in such work come 'naturally' to women and, therefore, need no monetary compensation or recognition. It is believed that women's contribution to the standard of living of other family members depends not only on their ability to earn an income, but on the time they commit to emotional and domestic care of household members. Consequently, while women in paid labour with family commitments may spend less time during weekdays on these tasks, they spend an average of five hours a day on housework during weekends. This represents twice the time of their husbands (Fletcher, 1978).

The Practices of Female Culture

Men's pursuit of male mateship grows out of the organization of men's lives around paid labour. For women, the lack of economic resources, restrictions on geographic mobility, and the continual demands on women's time, all of which are associated with living within one's workplace (the home), means that the pursuit of mateship is replaced by the pursuit of a familial ideal. The presentation of home, children, and husband becomes the preoccupation, and self-sacrifice becomes as much ritualized in female culture as mateship is in male.

Female culture becomes essentially 'meeting others' needs'. Despite the frequent assertion of the equality of their marriage relationships, the women in James' study of Kawerau recognized that familial needs virtually absorbed them. One commented:

Sometimes I feel as though I'm sitting on the sideline watching the other people getting on with their lives. . . I'm the one that makes lunch and takes the children along and sits and waits for him to finish enjoying himself out there and comes home and cleans up after it. (James, 1985: 115-16.)

Part of this culture, then, consists of a mentality of vicarious living. Another woman in James' (1985: 115-16) study asserted:

And then you have children. Well the most important thing is to try and bring those children up because its their future. . . your life is finished now. . . help those children so they can get something behind them when they grow up.

Associated with this ritualization of sacrifice is a deflation in women's expectations of men.

The obligations to women and children that men are expected to fulfil within marriage are often practically non-existent. One of *The Smith Women* (a hundred women with the surname Smith, interviewed by Barrington and Gray) described the dynamics of her marriage:

Money was very bad. Many a time we had to have weetbix or porridge one whole day because he used to drink his money away. If I could get him straight after pay day I could usually get some money out of him. But in the end he got to like his drink too much. He was a good husband — he never beat us or anything like that. (Barrington and Gray, 1981: 153.)

This woman explained her eventual divorce from this man as largely a lack of communication exacerbated by her husband's mother, not in terms of any material hardship:

He always talked to his mother first and she would advise him and then I would say something and I was always wrong. So you'd get the old triangle thing. (Barrington and Gray, 1981: 153.)

This may be an extreme example, but research repeatedly shows that even women, committed to a division of labour between the sexes in which the male is the breadwinner and women are full-time wives and mothers in the home, consider the wage a man's property, as opposed to a family wage. Men frequently retain the right to decide the portion of the wages given to women for the maintenance of the household. Women are very reluctant to ask for more, or to spend 'household' money on themselves (Barrington and Gray, 1981: 87-9; James, 1985: 237-56).

This ritual of self-sacrifice directly connects the motifs of Dependent Woman and Moral Redemptress. Indeed, sacrifice mediates to some extent the contradictions between the two. Of course, sacrifice is a central feature of women's lives simply by virtue of the economic dependency embedded in female culture. However, sacrifice also provides an opportunity for women to grasp a modicum of power by the assertion of their superiority.

Female selflessness, as opposed to male selfishness, is celebrated by women of widely differing politics. Conservative women promote it by seeking to maintain a female culture as it is constituted through the Cult of Domesticity. Cultural feminists also seek to assert allegedly 'life-giving', innately female values over allegedly innately male, destructive values, which they argue dominate our society today (Cox and James, 1987: 13; Segal, 1987: 3). The assertion of women as Moral Redemptress works at both the level of women's everyday lives and at the more lofty heights of political debate and social policy. The notion of woman as Moral Redemptress has been particularly pertinent in continuing debate over pornography. Some even suggest that women should dominate the appointments to statutory bodies regulating the sale and distribution of pornographic material. This is partly because women are seen as the victims of pornography, and therefore should have the right to protect themselves through controlling pornography. This is also argued on the basis of women's alleged moral superiority to men. However, perhaps the clearest expression of women as Moral Redemptress in private life is the tendency for many women to remain in situations of repetitive domestic violence.

Essential to keeping women in violent situations is the association of femininity with moral authority and leadership. Repeatedly, research into the motives underlying the actions of women who are victims of domestic violence has pointed to women's feelings of responsibility. This consists not merely of feelings of guilt for 'triggering' violent outbursts, but also the belief that it is their responsibility as women to 'tame', reform, or control their husbands. This embodies an underlying assertion of women's moral superiority over men. It implies that women are needed by the very individuals who perpetrate violence against them (Dean, 1979: 10; Jackson, 1978: 27). There is not very much difference between this position and the joking among women about men's domestic incompetency.

Of course, there are many reasons why women remain in violent domestic situations. One of the most compelling is economic dependency. Jackson (1978: 26), who surveyed over 200 battered wives in New Zealand, found that nearly one-third returned within a few weeks because, with limited finances, they could not survive. However, despite the effects of economic dependency and limited earning power within paid labour, some women do leave their partners and, in doing so, many accept the stigmatization and the extreme poverty associated with solo parenthood (Saville-Smith, 1987a: 200-8). Of those who suffer domestic violence and remain, many are simply too fearful to get out. Others with children consider that to leave would be too disturbing for their children, despite the negative effects of marital violence on their children which they report (Jackson, 1978: 27).

The assertion of moral superiority associated with the role of mother has provided women with a social influence which far exceeds their economic power. For many women, the rewards are largely symbolic, however. Despite this, when confronted with the structures of exclusion in paid labour, and the exploitative nature of much of women's paid work, it is hardly surprising that many women actively maintain female culture. Many accept dependency as a privilege. Some actively work against the renegotiation of the structures of paid and unpaid work, the redistribution of economic, political, and social resources, and the reconstruction of concepts of femininity. The moral right, in particular, has provided a vehicle for women to express such sentiments (*Broadsheet*, 1985; Ryan, 1986).

However, it is not just women active in the moral right who are fearful of the challenges posed to traditional gender relations by liberal social policy and feminism. The moral right has tapped real insecurities and anxieties which people have about family life (Ryan, 1986: 111). *The Smith Women* identified primarily with their families, and were clearly hostile to feminist ideas (Barrington and Gray, 1981: 194-5). Like these women, some of the women in James' (1985: 216) study viewed any move away from domesticity as potentially undermining their feminine identity and power. Yet the problems created for women in particular and, indeed, for all members of society by the internal dynamics of male and female cultures make a reassertion of traditional femininity both impractical and dangerous. The costs of the gendered culture to our society are enormous.

1 Rituals are formal and routinized actions which are predominantly symbolic. That is, they are designed to express particular meanings recognizable to members of the group or culture.

2 The activity of drinking and then driving is not confined to men, nor is it necessarily ritualized behaviour. Because drinking is often done away from the home in pubs, at parties, or at the workplace, many people do in fact drive after drinking simply to return home. It is not these actions we are examining, but rather, ritualized drinking and driving where men combine these activities specifically to assert their masculinity and control over their environment. This is often done even though others, often wives and girlfriends, are sober and available to drive for them.

3 From fieldwork undertaken by James (1985).

The Costs of a Gendered Culture

The gendered culture of contemporary New Zealand was constructed in the context of social unrest in the late nineteenth century. The popular debates of the 1880s surrounded issues which today seem familiar: violence, destitution, vagrancy, gangs, juvenile delinquency, crime, and the sexual exploitation of women. The promotion of the Cult of Domesticity and the development of notions of the Family Man and the Man Alone were attempts to resolve those problems. A century later, the solution, the gendered culture, has become a significant part of the problem.

Since 1979, various policy documents, committees, commissions, and hearings have considered problems of disorder ranging from gangs, violent offending, and sexual abuse to our extraordinarily high road death toll. Few have analysed these problems within the context of our gendered culture. The *Roper Report* (Ministerial Committee of Inquiry into Violence, 1987), for instance, not only committed fewer than ten pages to considering domestic violence, but made little attempt to analyse the gender structures which inform family life.

Violence within the family was portrayed by the Committee of Inquiry into Violence (1987: 99-100) as being restricted to pathologically disturbed or high-risk families in which violence might be triggered by anything from women's unwillingness 'to accept their traditional role in the home', to media images of the 'distinctions between rich and poor' which generate 'feelings of envy, shame and frustration'. Indeed, the committee provides a smorgasbord of explanations, presumably hoping that in a large menu everyone will find something to please them.

Throughout the report, the fact that violence is perpetrated almost entirely by men is mentioned, yet hardly considered. The only real exploration of gender or gender relations in this report, which was presented as the most definitive inquiry into violence in our society, was to be found in a desultory discussion of advertising. In this, the committee (1987: 58) concluded that:

> . . . some advertising is sexist in the sense that it tends to devalue women, or women's role in the community . . . Such advertising does not instill respect for women . . . some liquor advertising, and particularly beer advertising is at fault for its promotion of macho values which have no part in a caring community . . .

Clearly, the *Roper Report* constitutes a public recognition that masculinity is somehow connected to male anti-social behaviour. But images are identified as 'The Problem', rather than the structures and social relations through which images are expressed.

Resistance to confronting the structure of male culture reflects a contradiction between the way our society eulogizes masculinity to the point that it is almost synonymous with national identity and, simultaneously, having to admit that social problems do emerge from specific aspects of masculinity. To question masculinity is to be critical of our national ethos. To examine the costs of male culture is to imply that all men participate in the social disorders which we, as a society, presently confront. In a sense, however, to examine male culture critically is more acceptable than suggesting that costs may accrue from the internal workings of female culture. This is partly because women tend to be the victims of male anti-social behaviour, and partly because female culture is closely identified with morality, stability, and idealized family life.

Within male culture, the motif of the Man Alone signals the potential disruptiveness of men. However, portraying female culture, as it is expressed in the Cult of Domesticity, as socially dangerous is almost unthinkable. Nevertheless, there is little doubt that costs accrue not simply from male culture, or even from the interface between male and female cultures, but also from female culture itself. Female culture, as it is constituted through the Cult of Domesticity, throws up social costs which fall on women and on society as a whole. In this chapter, we examine the price of a gendered culture which leads to the wastage of human resources and demands expensive interventions by both the State and other agencies. Nowhere is such waste so obvious as in men's abuse of alcohol.

Men and Alcohol Abuse

Alcohol abuse is a major public health problem in New Zealand. It contributes to illness and deaths, motor accidents, lost production, and violent offences. Alcohol abuse as a public health problem derives in a large part from the social construction of masculinity in general, and male drinking patterns in particular. The practice of drinking to excess, as part of men's expression of mateship and the testing of masculinity, the rituals which combine alcohol with driving, and alcohol's role in violent behaviour, not only threaten individual life but confront the public with a huge health bill.

The total number of people who abuse alcohol is not known. In New

Zealand, there are an estimated 53,000 chronic alcoholics (Department of Statistics, 1987: 173), but alcohol is abused by a far wider number than just these individuals. The Alcohol Liquor Advisory Council's national survey estimated that over 212,500 people drink heavily (Management Services and Research Unit, 1983: 108). The majority of those who abuse alcohol and who are directly affected by alcohol-associated illness and death are men.

Approximately 75 per cent of chronic alcoholics are male (Rayner *et al.*, 1984: 48). In 1985, the alcohol death rate for men was 82 per million mean population, compared to only 18 per million for women (National Health Statistics Centre, 1985: 15). Furthermore, drink-driving offences are mostly perpetrated by males who make up 90.5 per cent of the offenders (Bailey and Allo, 1987: 9).

Many others, not themselves excessive drinkers, are also affected by alcohol abuse. For every chronic alcoholic, an estimated ten others — family, friends, and workmates — are also affected (Department of Statistics, 1986: 173). Even if only the economic costs to society are calculated the costs of alcohol abuse are enormous. Rayner *et al.* (1984: 7) conservatively assess the economic costs of alcohol abuse in New Zealand to be between 2.7 and 3.4 per cent of the gross national product (GNP) ($787.9 million-$974.9 million) in 1981-1982. At around 3 per cent GNP, these costs are not far short of the 5.3 per cent of GNP spent on education in 1982 (Department of Statistics, 1984a: 217).

Increases in alcohol consumption and the death rate from alcohol-related causes are closely connected. Over the period 1967-1978, when alcohol consumption increased, the death rate from alcohol-related causes trebled (Management Services and Research Unit, 1983: 106). Individuals who drink heavily are prone to illness and possible death from cirrhosis of the liver, alcoholic gastritis, alcoholic cardiomyopathy, alcoholic psychosis, alcoholic dependence syndrome, accidents, and alcoholic poisoning (National Health Statistics Centre, 1985: 15). The consequences of alcohol abuse put a major strain on the resources of general hospitals, both public and private, and are related to an increasing proportion of psychiatric hospital admissions (Management Services and Research Unit, 1983: 106-7). The psychiatric care of chronic alcoholics is never likely to be undertaken by the private health sector.

By far the greatest cost of alcohol abuse is, according to Rayner *et al.* (1984), in lost production (2-2.7 per cent GNP). Decreased efficiency, absenteeism, and the loss of workers from the labour force are all associated with alcohol abuse. The costs connected to alcohol-related crime, accidents, fire and to social responses such as treatment, rehabilitation, public education, and training of personnel have never been calculated. Drinking-driving, however, has always been recognized as a major social problem and here the costs have been calculated.

One study has suggested that New Zealand has a greater number of alcohol-related traffic accidents than any other country (Simpson, 1984: 265). Another study found that about half of the fatal road accidents involve excess alcohol consumption, and 20 per cent of hospitalized drivers have been drinking (Bailey and Allo, 1987: 5). Every year about 300 lives are lost due to drinking and driving. The total cost is conservatively estimated at about $110 million (Bailey, 1986: 1). This would be considerably more if the costs of the Ministry of Transport's operation and the courts were included. In one year, the greater Wellington area alone produces almost 3800 drink-drive convictions (Bailey and Allo, 1987: 5).

The practice of drinking and driving cannot be understood without reference to male culture. Men are far more likely than women to drink and drink heavily, and are thus greatly over-represented in drink-driving statistics. Just as alcohol is an important component of masculine activities, so too are machines associated with masculinity. They become an extension of the body, symbolizing strength, skill, control, and virility:

> . . . the desire for skill and force of the body is translated into a preoccupation with technology and speed. . . Cars and bikes give an amplified way of occupying space and putting one's impress upon it. (Connell, 1983: 23.)

The combination of vehicles and alcohol is particularly important for young New Zealand men aspiring to masculinity, and it is very destructive. Males under twenty-five years of age constitute almost 41 per cent of fatal road accidents involving drinking drivers (Bailey and Allo, 1987: 21).

The strong association between alcohol and violence must also be understood in terms of male mateship behaviour. Bradbury (1984: 65) shows that 60 per cent of those involved in violent offending had been drinking and the great majority of offenders are men. More importantly, violence does not occur simply as a result of drinking, but as a consequence of the drinking location:

> Violence appeared to be accepted as a more appropriate response to certain situations in the pub milieu than in other social contexts. . . the almost nonchalant way in which [the offenders] reported violent incidents which had happened in the pub, or originated in the pub, indicated that such behaviour was being viewed as an integral part of the pub environment. (Bradbury, 1984: 83.)

There appears, then, to be a strong relationship between the male environment of the pub and violent behaviour in general. However, although it is almost entirely a male activity, perpetrated by males and against males, violence is not confined to the pub.

Male Mateship: a culture of violence

In 1985, almost 89 per cent of all violent offences reported to the police were committed by men (New Zealand Police, 1986: 10). A focus on violent offending, however, obscures the widespread and institutionalized nature of violence in male culture. Nowhere is this more apparent than in sport. Rugby, arguably the most masculine of sports in New Zealand because of its physicality, is also one which is persistently implicated in discussion of sports violence. This violence is not unusual. It occurs routinely during legitimate play and often results in serious accidents, involving spinal and head injuries and death.

In rugby, the line between aggressive tactics and dirty play is frequently blurred. This is promoted by a masculinity in which one is expected both to 'hand it out' and 'take it' in the tradition of Colin Meads (Phillips, 1987: 125). Thus, injuries also become the mark of masculinity, as 'trophies' to be prized (Kedgley, 1985: 30). Pressure to prove manhood through physical endurance extends to after-match activities. Drinking games and explicitly violent confrontations such as 'argy-bargy' continue the aggression of competition off the sports field.

Substantial financial costs accrue from the institutionalization of violence in sport. Apart from the obvious costs to individuals, society as a whole pays. In 1984, just over 16,000 sporting injuries cost the Accident Compensation Commission almost $13 million, 11 per cent of the total compensation paid out for injuries that year (Department of Statistics, 1986: 29).

Violence is a key feature of male culture, in part because it proves one's masculinity to other men and expresses male solidarity. It is also an important means of exercising power and authority over women and children in the home. This is particularly true when other more legitimate expressions of male authority prove ineffective.

Violence as an Instrument of Male Authority

Violence within the home was referred to in the *Roper Report* as a 'problem of frightening proportions' (Ministerial Committee, 1987: 96), but its widespread incidence is only gradually being recognized. Statistics on the incidence of domestic violence against women are difficult to obtain, partly because an estimated 97 per cent of cases are not reported

(Police Submissions, 1986: 59). Furthermore, records of domestic violence against women are still not kept routinely by the Justice Department (Ministerial Committee of Inquiry, 1987: 96). This reflects the widespread view in our society that family privacy is sacrosanct and, in particular, that male authority in the home should not be challenged. These ideas were upheld by a court in a Palmerston North assault case in 1978 in which one man assaulted another in an effort to protect a woman from further beating. The defendant had not known that the woman was the complainant's wife and was consequently charged with assault. He was later told by the magistrate who fined him: 'That's what you get for poking your nose into other people's business' (cited in Social Development Council, 1980: 9).

Despite the inadequacy of the statistics, it is apparent that the number of reported domestic disputes[1] has risen substantially. This is not simply due to women speaking out about sexual abuse and violence which had been previously covered up; there appears to have been an actual increase in domestic violence against women since the early 1970s (Pratt, 1987: 41). Since 1978, when the police began to record incidents of domestic disputes, to 1985-1986, there has been an increase of 117 per cent (Pratt, 1987: 39). Over approximately the same time period, the police attended an annual average of more than 16,500 domestic disputes, but only an average of 285 charges were laid yearly (Ministerial Committee, 1987: 97).

Low rates of prosecution reflect the unwillingness of the police, until recently, to act formally on domestic disputes and the tendency to attempt to 'defuse' the situation rather than arrest the perpetrator (Ford, 1986; Social Development Council, 1980: 23-5). It also reflects the unwillingness of many women to lay charges against their husbands, lovers, or relatives. Whether or not charges are laid, the costs in police time alone are enormous. It is estimated that one-third of police calls concern domestic violence (Dean, 1979: 5). The costs of domestic violence to the 26,000 women estimated to be beaten every year (Ford, 1986: 3) are even greater.

For some, domestic violence culminates in death. One-third of all homicides are associated with domestic disputes (Ministerial Committee, 1987: 97). For those who do not die, psychological and physical damages demand large expenditures of collective resources, whether these are administered by the State or other agencies. Medical services must deal with physical injuries sustained in domestic violence, ranging from miscarriages to broken bones, damage to internal organs, bruising, lacerations, neurological damage, paralysis, and loss of sight and hearing (Social Development Council, 1980: 15-17). The effects on women's mental health have been less carefully enumerated, but it cannot be

Table 2: Marital Status and Sex of First Admissions to Psychiatric Hospitals 1983–1985

Year	Males (rates per 100,000 male population)		Females (rates per 100,000 female population)	
	Single	Married	Single	Married
1983	70.8	49.5	41.6	52.1
1984	66.9	45.2	41.3	48.8
1985*	71.4	41.9	45.2	49

*Provisional: year ending 31 March.
Source: National Health Statistics Centre, *Mental Health Data,* 1983, 1984, 1985.

entirely coincidental that while single women display the best mental health, as represented by first admissions to psychiatric hospitals, married women are worse off (Table 2). Whether a woman is physically abused or not, marriage appears to be a definite health risk for her. Among the psychological consequences of domestic violence are fear, anxiety, exhaustion, drug abuse, and suicide. All represent a wastage of human resources.

Costs are also borne by community agencies which provide substantial support for women experiencing domestic violence. Women's refuges offer temporary housing for some 1600 women and almost 3000 children each year (Ministerial Committee, 1987: 97). These services, being underdeveloped and receiving only limited funding from central Government, are unable to cope with the great demand for help. Furthermore, while the police often give advice when attending domestic disputes, they do not have the training to offer counselling and mediation (Ford, 1986: 25). The development of services for victims is an area of potential expenditure which the Ministerial Committee of Inquiry into Violence (1987: 143) has recognized as necessary.

Rape, too, is a form of violence against women that is perpetrated both within and outside the home. The 'quiet Kiwi male' has the doubtful honour of being responsible for one of the top five rape rates in Western societies (*Evening Standard,* 2 May 1987: 3). The majority of rapes occur in domestic circumstances. *The Victims Survey* found 63 per cent of rapes took place within the home (Stone, Barrington, and Bevan, 1983: 9). Moreover, women are frequently raped by someone known to them. Over half of all rapes reported to the police came into this category in Stace's study (Stace, 1983: Appendix, Table 18). The physical and psychological costs of rape, in the way of injuries, trauma, and disruption to social relationships are well documented (Saville-Smith,

1987b: 6; Pow, 1986). The financial costs of rape to society, however, have not been calculated. Nevertheless, it is apparent that the meagre funding that Rape Crisis Centres receive does not meet the costs of their services. In addition the justice and health systems both incur costs in dealing with rape cases.

As well as women, we know that children, too, suffer from male violence. However, statistics on child assault are even harder to obtain than figures on domestic violence against women. The National Advisory Council for Child Abuse estimates twenty-five cases of child abuse per 100,000 children occur per year (Ministerial Committee, 1987: 97-8). Workers and researchers in the area agree that the reported cases of violence and sexual abuse against children represent only a small fraction of the real incidence. Studies suggest that men and women, more or less equally, physically abuse children (Social Development Council, 1980: 2), but child sexual abuse is overwhelmingly carried out by men (Von Dadelszen, 1987: 10). Children experiencing sexual abuse bear the costs personally through psychological and physical damage. They are vulnerable to a wide range of problems, including mood changes, nightmares, school problems, difficulties with interpersonal relationships, and suicidal feelings (Von Dadelszen, 1987: 13-17).

The economic costs of domestic violence to women and children can be measured in terms of the time and resources spent by the police in dealing with such incidents, the costs in establishing and maintaining services for victims, and the costs associated with court appearances and imprisonment for offenders. Other costs are almost impossible to calculate. These include, for women and children, the physical and psychological injuries endured. For society, the cost is that, for some, violence is an accepted part of social interaction (Bradbury, 1984: 94; Ministerial Committee, 1987: 98). This is not, contrary to media images, confined to any one ethnic group or class, but is a style of life, one that is in no small way condoned by the social construction of masculinity in our society. Domestic violence is a symptom of the structures in which male dominance is embedded.

Domestic abuse of women and children is an extension of the everyday acceptance of violence as a way of dealing with others, especially the powerless. For example, the widespread use of corporal punishment, both in the home and at some schools, illustrates the institutionalization of violence in our society as a means of expressing anger and controlling others. The Ritchies (1978: 103) found that only a very small percentage of parents reported never using corporal punishment.

While hitting a child is frequently a spontaneous response to anger and frustration, it also expresses the household's relations of power and authority, and becomes a significant way of maintaining them. James

(1985: 182) found that while the mothers in her study carried out routine disciplining of children, fathers were often used as the 'ultimate deterrent'. They stepped in to deal with serious infringements and thus confirmed their authority as head of the household. Although recognizing that disciplining children is one of the most problematical aspects of child-rearing, studies also indicate the inadequacy of corporal punishment. It is ultimately ineffective in changing children's behaviour, and merely fosters hostility and resentment. It places strain on both parents and children, and leads children to accept violence as a justified means of problem-solving and as a normal expression of emotion (Social Development Council, 1980: 21-3).

The acceptance of violence as 'normal' behaviour is borne out by Bradbury's (1984: 27) study of violent offenders who reported no remorse over their actions and felt the victim had deserved the injuries inflicted. Moreover, violent behaviour is not only condoned by violent offenders. A flood of newspaper coupons received by the Ministerial Committee of Inquiry into Violence (1987: 11) insisted on corporal punishment for violent and drug-related offences, and even capital punishment for murder and drug dealing.

Societal attitudes towards violence are ambiguous. On the one hand, violent offending is widely condemned. At the same time, severe punishment for criminal offences is advocated by some, and corporal punishment for children is accepted in many families and still in some parts of the educational system. Violence against women is not publicly condoned, but is nevertheless acknowledged as an almost inevitable part of private life. This is partly because violence against women has traditionally been associated with men's legitimate authority over women. It is also because vulnerability to violence is intrinsic to female culture. Women's impoverishment and dependence make them open to exploitation and domination by men, and outright physical abuse.

Female Culture: being the victim

The Cult of Domesticity, the female culture which defines women in terms of their child-bearing and rearing capacity, provides a rationale for the impoverishment of women. The personal impact of economic dependency is frequently unrecognized. Low wages in the workplace are accepted by young women as not only normal, but, because paid work itself is still perceived as largely a transitional stage in their life cycle, of no real concern. The costs of this are borne by those women, and there are increasing numbers of them, for whom wage labour is not a transitional phase between dependency as daughters to dependency as wives. Now, at least 35 per cent of married women are in full-time paid work, and at least 10 per cent have part-time jobs (Hall, 1987: 3, 7). Furthermore, increasing numbers of women are single and therefore cannot rely on a man for support. In 1981, over 41 per cent of women over fifteen years were 'not married'; that is, never married, separated, widowed, or divorced (Department of Statistics, 1987: 138). The costs of impoverishment fall on those who find, for whatever reason, the exchange between breadwinner and unpaid houseworker is either not established or has broken down. In the latter case, the reality of women's impoverishment is experienced with a vengeance.

Solo-parent families in New Zealand, of which the great majority are headed by women, are among the poorest households. In 1981, only just over half of solo-parent families owned their own homes compared to three-quarters of two-parent households. Of two-parent families, more than 90 per cent owned at least one car, while among solo-parent families, less than 75 per cent owned a car. Appliances and services from telephones to doctors, washing machines to dentists are luxuries for solo-parent families. The household maintained by the solo-mother confronts the most severe destitution. Of the families with incomes of less than $8,000 per annum in 1981, 50 per cent were headed by solo-women (Department of Statistics, 1986: 28-48).

In these households, it is not only women, but their children as well, who suffer the costs of female impoverishment. The costs are also borne by society as a whole. Women's limited opportunities in paid labour make them more likely than men to become dependent on the Welfare State. The State makes a considerable saving by supporting the structures of privatized child-rearing and women's dependency (Saville-Smith, 1987a: 196-207), but the over-representation of women among social welfare recipients directly reflects of the structural organization of female culture and the dependency it institutionalizes.

Finally, there are costs to mental health which emerge from the gendered culture. Economic dependency, domesticity, and the self-sacrifice demanded of women by the Cult of Domesticity are major causes of women's mental illness. Women are much more likely than men to be admitted to psychiatric institutions for neurotic depression and other depressive conditions and psychoses. All of these are linked to women's isolation and confinement to domesticity (Craig and Mills, 1987: 22). New Zealand studies identify two crucial 'at risk' periods in women's lives: the early years of motherhood and the end of mothering (Calvert, 1978; Thompson, 1977). It is in these periods that women most acutely experience the strains and conflicts of the maternal role as traditionally defined in our society.

In the child-bearing years, postpartum depression is a major cause of mental illness of women in New Zealand. It has been suggested that up to 21 per cent of women who are treated for mental illness can trace the first occurrence of that illness to soon after the birth of a child (Calvert, 1978: 9). Motherhood is a source of great stress for women in our society for many reasons. It often means a major change in a woman's position; from earning money, to dependence on a husband and being defined almost totally in terms of the child's needs. Feelings of loss of control and helplessness characterize the experience. In Calvert's study (1978: 9), many of the women interviewed commented on their lack of control over reproductive matters. More than half of first births in New Zealand are conceived outside marriage (Fergusson *et al.,* 1979). This is consonant with New Zealand's historically high ex-nuptial conception rates and reveals the extent to which women are trapped into motherhood and its responsibilities. Calvert (1978: 9) argues that feelings of lack of control and helplessness over reproduction have widespread consequences which extend to how women experience their relationships to their partners, friends, and others.

When children leave home, those women who have devoted themselves to full-time mothering frequently experience feelings of loss and a lack of meaning to their lives. Typically lacking in employment skills and confidence, they have neither their old home responsibilities, nor can they easily develop other avenues of fulfilment. Furthermore, their social worth is diminishing, simply because they are growing old:

These women look toward the next twenty years of their lives as older women in a society which does not value the old (especially older women) and as women whose role (of wife and mother) is no longer relevant. (Calvert, 1978: 9.)

This suggested relationship between the roles of wife and mother and poor mental health is confirmed by mental health statistics. Admission rates clearly show that more married than single women enter psychiatric hospitals (see Table 2).

A Gendered Culture: who pays?

Sandra Coney (1986) once asked in her newspaper column:

Can the country afford men? Can it afford the courts, prisons and borstals and police? Can it afford to have hospital services congested with long-term orthopedic patients smashed up on the roads, in pub carparks and rugby fields? The cost of the invisible injuries is harder to assess. Who can put a price on the pain of the child victim of father-rape?

However, these costs do not derive from the dynamics of male culture alone. Major social costs also arise from female culture. Most importantly, the gendered culture, in which male and female cultures are interfaced, imposes costs on men as well as women. Nor should one characterize, as Coney does, male culture as just being about men's domination over women. If one considers mental health data more closely (see Table 2), it is certainly clear that marriage is much healthier for men than it is for women. Married men enjoy consistently better mental health than single males. This undoubtedly reflects the benefits men derive from women's domestic services. Embedded in these statistics are other inequalities, however. They reflect the struggles that go on between men.

The Man Alone — the single man — is still a problem for social order. In contrast to women, men are over-represented in admissions for alcohol dependence and abuse. Furthermore, men overall are more likely to be admitted to a psychiatric institution (Craig and Mills, 1987: 22). Unfortunately, we do not know, owing to the nature of statistical data, the class positions of those admitted to psychiatric hospitals. We do know, however, that those admissions reflect the structure of inequalities of race in New Zealand. Of all men, Māori men have the highest rates of admission (Figure 1). For Māori, both men and women, psychiatric institutions are not places of retreat in which to manage illness, but an agency of social control. Māori are more than twice as likely to be referred to a psychiatric institution by law-enforcement agencies as are non-Māori (Craig and Mills, 1987: 23).

Figure 1: Admissions to Institutions for the Mentally Ill — Rates by Ethnicity and Sex, 1977–1984.

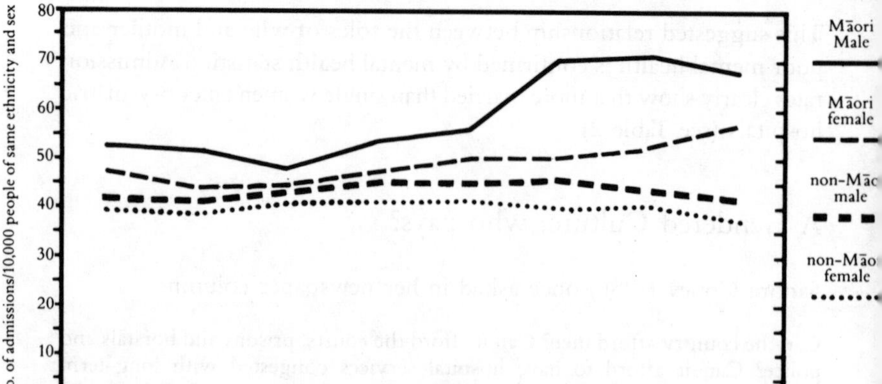

Note: Rates do not include admissions attributable to intellectual handicap.
Sources: Department of Health, *Mental Health Data* 1977–1984.
Department of Statistics, *Population Estimates* 1977–1984.

To summarize, our discussion demonstrates three important points. Firstly, that a gendered culture derives not simply from sex hierarchies but is also a response to, and reflects, the interests of those who dominate other structures of inequality. Secondly, and in consequence, the costs of a gendered culture fall on both men and women. Finally, that while the costs of a gendered culture fall on society as a whole, it falls more heavily on some than on others. Women are especially affected, through violence towards themselves and their children and economic dependence. Furthermore, because they are expected to be the main care-givers in families and communities, women deal with the consequences of alcohol abuse, accidents, and violence much more directly than men. They are more likely than men to be in a position of having to support an alcoholic. They care for the ill and disabled and they provide community services for victims of male violence.

However, wage and salary earners also have to bear the costs of systems of intervention. Even if the State gave up many of its other services, it would still have to provide support for the victims of violence, abuse, and impoverishment. These services will never be supplied by the private sector because they are unprofitable. Yet they are crucial to the maintenance of a social order which benefits all. Under these circumstances, the working class not only pays for its own welfare (Bedggood, 1980: 96), but also subsidizes those with productive property and capital. Polynesians, particularly Māori, predominately fall into unpropertied low-income categories, and therefore are especially burdened by these costs. They also face the added burden of racism. They are frequently made the scapegoats for the problems which actually emanate from the gendered culture. Clearly, then, to be able to confront and diminish the costs of the gendered culture, one must consider the nature and structure of those groups with and without a vested interest in its maintenance.

1 'Domestic Dispute' is defined by the police as:

a complaint relating to a situation involving family members, people living together or nearby each other, where the police are called to restore order or to act as mediators. (Ford, 1986: 3.)

Thus conflict between relatives may be included in police figures as well as male assaults on their female partners. However, it appears that the majority of domestic disputes involve men and women who are currently, or have been, in a marital relationship.

Vested Interests in a Gendered Culture

Why is it that the gendered culture is vigorously maintained when it results in so many costs for individuals and for society as a whole? Women obviously bear many of its costs: sexual abuse and violence, impoverishment and having to deal with the effects of others' alcohol and drug abuse. Working-class and Polynesian[1] men are also disproportionately affected by the adverse consequences of alcohol abuse, violence, and the public sanctions placed on the aspects of male culture which are deemed to be anti-social. Nevertheless, even those who bear many of its costs act, frequently quite consciously and purposively, to maintain at least the symbols of a gendered culture.

The answer to why a gendered culture maintains itself revolves around three issues. The first of these is a conflation in the popular mind of sex and gender. Secondly, even those groups who are disadvantaged by the gendered culture can use it, in certain contexts, to expand their limited access to power and resources. Thirdly, the gendered culture offers benefits to those in dominant positions in the hierarchies of race, class, and sex, respectively.

Nature and the Gendered Culture

Masculinity and femininity are popularly regarded as natural and immutable arrangements. Any change is frequently seen as creating problems. Suggestions that women should develop a career or men take responsibility for domestic tasks or child-rearing is taken to threaten the basis of social order. These fears directly reflect the belief that the family is the basic unit of all societies and, more particularly, that 'normal' family life inevitably involves a sexual division of labour such as that presently constituted within our gendered culture.'Even Treasury (1987: 122) has announced that while it regards all other social relations as contracts made between freely motivated individuals, families arise unconsciously and exhibit a 'natural cohesion'.

Such beliefs bring about some of the most extraordinary conceptual twists and turns among those attempting to confront the problems of familial violence. For example, the Committee of Inquiry into Violence (1987: 99) noted that:

It was questioned whether it is possible in the highly complex and technological society in which we live, for two parents, let along a solo-parent, as is increasingly the case, to provide for the material, emotional and social needs of their children and their own relationships.

Given that violence in families is so frequently committed by men in nuclear families, the implication that solo-parent families (which are predominantly female-headed) are even less able to provide for emotional and social needs seems rather odd. Certainly, solo-parents are materially impoverished, but political will could resolve that situation. Embodied in this comment is a refusal, despite all the evidence, to accept that solo-parent families may not only be appropriate familial structures but an improvement on supposedly natural, heterosexual parental relations.

The inappropriateness of an uncritical commitment to the nuclear family has been discussed at length elsewhere (Hall, 1987; James, 1986; Koopman-Boyden & Scott, 1984). It is a commitment that derives from the popular belief that an individual's physiology determines their personal qualities and their social roles. This is a convenient belief because it protects a gendered culture which expresses and maintains the systematic structuring of inequalities in our society. The gendered culture both works to provide the disadvantaged in these systems with a stake in the organization of our society, and it benefits dominant groups directly. The following discussion is an attempt to expose the mechanisms through which the gendered culture maintains the inequalities of race, class, and sex.

Maintaining Inequalities of Race

The gendered culture maintains inequalities of race in complex and sometimes contradictory ways. On the one hand, it brings together men of different racial and ethnic[2] groups. On the other hand, it emphasizes the common 'race interests' of men and women in the dominant racial group (that is, the Pākehā).

Male mateship, through its egalitarian ethos, ideally extends comradeship to all men, irrespective of class or racial distinctions. With regard to race, this is often expressed in an idealized way which asserts the successful assimilation of the Māori into white society. Popular legends of assimilation emphasize the significant participation of Māori men in rugby and their prowess in wars in Europe. Māori achievements in these spheres have been praised by men prominent in both Māori and Pākehā societies (Phillips, 1987: 287). However, the real extent of Māori acceptance into New Zealand society is somewhat different.

John Rangihau argues that, in reality, Māori have had a limited involvement in, and even less access to, the privileges of the Pākehā world. The idea of male 'comradeship' in sport and leisure conceals Māori confinement to an inferior social and economic position and their isolation from Pākehā and each other:

Unfortunately the areas where Maoris congregate are places like the local pubs or the racecourses. That, to me, is an indictment of our total society; these are the only places where Maoris feel they are on the eyeball to eyeball level with the rest of New Zealand society. (Rangihau, 1975: 223.)

Thus, the apparent egalitarianism of male mateship not only glosses over the real conditions of deprivation and racism experienced by the Māori, but it is also an expression of it. It obscures the fact that Pākehā males, who, in sport, may be 'just one of the boys', overwhelmingly control the economic and political institutions of our society.

The notion that Māori and Pākehā men participate equally in sport is more apparent than real. From yachting to rugby, sport is being increasingly sponsored, and thus controlled, by corporate interests. These companies are concerned with supporting activities consistent with their social sphere of operation and compatible with their public image. Providing funding for a Polynesian youth club, for instance, is simply not as 'rewarding' as mounting the America's Cup challenge.

Another significant source of funding for sport is the State, but there are substantial inequalities in the State's allocation of sport and recreation funds. This has been recognized with regard to women's sporting and recreational activities which still suffer from inadequate funding. However, certain men's organizations confront limited funding opportunities particularly when they cater for lower socio-economic groups. Both Polynesian and Pākehā working-class men are disadvantaged because of the individual costs of leisure. Sports such as skiing, hang-gliding, parachuting, golfing, and yachting are exclusive, simply because of the expenses associated with them (Simpson, 1984: 252-4). Moreover, Māori are, despite the Māori All Blacks, under-represented in organized sporting participation. Under these circumstances, even the notion of equality between Māori and Pākehā in sport and leisure, let alone in other spheres, becomes suspect. The 1981 Springbok Tour was significant precisely because it confronted the myth of egalitarian sport with the reality of institutionalized racism.

By no means are all male mateship collectivities approved of in our society. This is, in part, due to the inherent tensions in male culture between its two significant motifs, the Man Alone and the Family Man. It is also, in part, due to the threat that some male groups pose to Pākehā, rather than male, élites. Consequently, the distinctions between those mateship groups which are accepted and those which are not, are frequently made on racial lines rather than on the basis of behaviour.

Thus, while gangs are both a Pākehā and Polynesian phenomenon, public protest against gangs is shaped by the association made between gangs and Polynesians. Rhetoric about Pākehā and Polynesian being 'one people' is certainly not pursued when it comes to gangs. The word 'gang' has become so synonymous with Polynesian membership that the term 'ethnic gang' is used in official reports even when referring to gang activities in general (Ministerial Committee, 1987: 87).

In New Zealand, for many people crime is perceived as an ethnic phenomenon. That is, crime is regarded as an expression of particular Māori and Pacific Island cultural practices. These cultural practices are, in turn, frequently believed to be connected with genetic or racial characteristics. The perception of crime as an ethnic phenomenon obscures the close relationship between economic disadvantage and crime rates, and certain racist practices within the justice system.

Examples of institutional racism may be found in the procedures through which offenders' ethnic origins are recorded for statistical purposes. Often judgements are made regarding an offender's ethnicity or race by the police, rather than from the individual offender's stated ethnicity (Ministerial Committee, 1987: 41-2). Simpson (1979: 254) provides further evidence of institutional racism. In summarizing the literature, he found that a Māori is twice as likely to be sent to gaol as a Pākehā, and three times more likely as a Pākehā of the same socio-economic status. Such statistics indicate how many of our institutions systematically disadvantage non-Pākehā groups.

The idea that Polynesians are criminals is strong in the popular mind. Even the police submitted to the Ministerial Committee of Inquiry into Violence that: 'one of the most important keys to successfully reducing violent crimes is to reduce Maori offending' (Police Submissions, 1986: 27). However, it should be noted that while law-breaking by Māori is frequently considered a 'crime', law-breaking by Pākehā is less likely to be labelled as such. For instance, Ballara (1986: 144) found that in activities such as fraud and embezzlement, Pākehā are over-represented. These crimes are virtually ignored in law and order debates.

In a similar vein, the Hotel Association, which makes its profits from male conviviality, stated that young Māori people believe themselves to be above 'white man's law' (cited in Pratt, 1987: 15). Some members of Parliament have also posed the problem as if 'gangs', 'young thugs', and 'Māori crime' are inherently connected (Pratt, 1987: 15-16). Pratt's (1987) review of popular discourse on crime clearly illustrates that the distinctions between Polynesians (both Pacific Islanders and Māori), gangs, and youth are by no means clear in the law and order debate. All are blamed for the decay of a secure and moral society and all are seen as a threat to the authority of society's élite.

In short, whereas male mateship behaviour among Pākehā is usually accepted, the same group behaviour among Polynesians is regarded as intrinsically criminal and in need of constant surveillance. The solutions to disorder offered by the police reflect this suspicion that the everyday life of the Polynesian male is fundamentally criminal. They have demanded selective measures against specific groups, such as preventive detention for violent or sex offenders between twenty-one and twenty-five years of age and, more tellingly, for greater manpower and technological resources, such as electronic surveillance to combat alleged organized crime by gangs and a loosening of procedural and evidential regulations (Pratt, 1987: 19-21).

The notion that male mateship among Māori and Pacific Islanders leads to violent behaviour establishes the conditions for alliances between Pākehā men and women. Concern with Pākehā women's vulnerability to attack from strangers is a significant theme in the current portrayal of Polynesian males as the most violent members of New Zealand society. Inevitably, calls to 'make the streets safe' focus on visible groups such as the young, gangs, and Polynesians. Such demands are particularly vociferous when the public is shocked by something like a gang rape.

Gang rapes are frequently reported in a lurid and sensationalist fashion (Pratt, 1987: 31). Because Polynesians and gangs are conflated in the popular imagination, these reports, which focus on extreme examples of male violence, both cover up routine violence perpetrated by Pākehā men and reinforce the widespread assumption that most violence is committed by Polynesians. The reality is that male violence is more common in the home than on the streets. Furthermore, statistics show that in absolute terms a woman is more likely to be sexually assaulted by a Pākehā male than a Polynesian male (Department of Statistics, 1984b: 31).

The promotion of the idea that Polynesians are the cause of the alarming rise in violence makes women more concerned for their safety. Their response is to increase their commitment to 'rules of avoidance' (Saville-Smith, 1987b: 3-5) and limit their behaviour, movement, and freedom of association. These rules do not, in fact, protect women because the situations, behaviour, and activities which they imply are dangerous are, overall, less dangerous than staying at home. Most rape victims are raped by a man known to them or in the confines of their own homes, not by the mythical Polynesian wandering the streets at night. Because of the constraints of inter-ethnic contact, Pākehā women are most likely to be raped by Pākehā men. Rape is an act more likely to be perpetrated within ethnic groups than across them (Saville-Smith, 1987b: 4).

By focusing on minority ethnic groups as a threat to 'white

womanhood', Pākehā men have been able to maintain power over both women and other ethnic groups. Historically, the Pākehā promoted the protection of their women as an important rationalization for restrictions on Asian immigration. For example, cartoons in 1920, the year of the Immigration Restriction Act, highlighted fears of miscegenation as a justification for tightening immigration laws (Grant, 1980: 128-9).

Currently, definitions of Polynesian males as violent offenders, which imply a specific threat to Pākehā women, target these men for the repressive attention of the State through the justice system. Thus, women's legitimate concerns about their safety are co-opted by interests intent on preserving white power and authority. The real interests of women, of all ethnic groups, in freedom of movement, freedom from violence, and in controlling their sexuality are ignored. Bourne (1984: 13), reflecting on the experiences of the feminist movement in Britain, observes how women's responses to male violence may in fact reinforce oppression based on race:

In their failure to understand. . . women fail to side with the blacks; in failing to side with the blacks, they play into the hands of the state. Take, for example, one aspect of state racism in Britain today. In order to justify police harassment of the black community and the demand for increased police powers, the state is, through the media, highlighting 'mugging' — a term used to criminalise the black community: black youth are all muggers, their victims all white women. If we keep silent, appearing to concur with this view, we become in effect a party to state racism. Furthermore, because as feminists we have been campaigning against male violence on the streets, we can, if we do not consistently attack this type of stereotyping, even as we fight male violence actually give racism credibility.

The stereotype of the Polynesian rapist also conceals the sexual exploitation of women of minority ethnic groups by men of dominant cultures. In the United States:

. . . the portrayal of Black men as rapists reinforces racism's open invitation to white men to avail themselves sexually of Black women's bodies. The fictional image of the Black man as rapist has always strengthened its inseparable companion: the image of the Black woman as chronically promiscuous. (Davis, 1982: 182.)

In New Zealand the situation is similar. From the early days of contact between Māori and European, Māori women were viewed as naturally alluring. Joseph Banks wrote in 1770 of coquettish Māori women and, later, colonial photographers portrayed 'Māori beauties' bare-breasted to convey their alleged natural sensuality (King, 1983: 21). Such photographs reveal a stereotyped and patronizing view of the Māori. Clearly, Māori women were regarded as different from European women. Pictures of bare-breasted European women were not widely circulated, because it was unacceptable to portray European womanhood as primarily sexual. But Māori women were given no such respect and Māori women in erotic poses were popular pictorial subjects (King, 1983: 2). Throughout the early colonial period, Māori women were seen as natural prostitutes (Eldred-Grigg, 1984: 13, 28), while European prostitutes were considered to be women fallen from a position of original purity.

In essence the gendered culture displaces the issue of racism and subverts socially constructed inequalities by appealing to differences which are presented as natural. In our examination of the social understanding of violence and crime in our society, we have argued that these are assumed to be associated with Polynesians. Underlying this construction is a perception of the Pākehā as 'naturally' more law-abiding, less violent, and overall, as morally superior.

While all Pākehā gain benefits from the exclusion of Māori and Pacific Islanders from the control and consumption of resources, particular benefits accrue to those who own productive property and organize production in our society according to the dictates of profit. For business and farming interests, the dispossession of the Māori from their lands and resources has been a significant means of ensuring economic dominance. Equally, the maintenance of a large, relatively flexible pool of Pacific Island and Māori labour has been central to capital's ability to manage, expand, and contract its labour force requirements without being confronted with collective social resistance.

Maintaining Class Inequalities

Masculine and feminine cultures simultaneously support the ideology of egalitarianism in New Zealand while providing a mechanism by which class and associated structures of status[3] are reproduced. Inequalities in status, expressed through different lifestyles, are not perceived as *real* inequalities embedded in the organization of production in New Zealand (Chrisp, 1986). Rather, they tend to be seen, on the one hand, as superficial, almost frivolous, expressions of innate feminine tendencies, and, on the other, as an outgrowth of natural differences in intelligence, ability, or moral character.

The realities of economic inequalities are glossed over by attributing concerns about class position and status to women. This simultaneously affirms egalitarianism among men by implying that they are united at a deeper level than can be affected by mere class differences, while accentuating differences between men and women. In contrast to men, women are seen as isolated, socially competitive, and status conscious.

Oxley (1978: 95), in his study of two Australian towns, makes the observation that:

... groups which bring the strata together in interpersonal interaction are, for the most part, men's groups. And the virtues stressed in egalitarian ideologies. . . are virtues of masculinity. Egalitarianism seems very closely connected with the expression of male solidarity and superiority — of a tie which cuts across strata. Sex separation thus supports such an ideology.

In New Zealand, divisions between the sexes are similarly integral to egalitarianism. The following conversation among wives of mill workers in Kawerau,[4] exposes precisely the strong association of status-seeking and class-creating actions with women, and the denial of men's different class interests, and their pursuit of status.

Speaker 1 — [my husband] belongs to the golf club and it's really neat to see all the different guys together, you know, right from the labourers right up to the management. And they all get together.
Speaker 2 — Their game is golf. They're not like women, they're not cliquey.
Speaker 1 — They're not class mad. They've got no social distinction at all. They all get together and play golf. . . You know we've got the bank manager next door and he hardly talks to us at all. But at the golf club he's just like anybody else.
Speaker 3 — One of the boys.

These women accept as natural the egalitarianism among men. Yet further investigation shows that egalitarianism is little more than an ideal. It is absent among men on the mill site at Kawerau, and in the neighbourhood. In the mill, the workforce, which is almost exclusively male, is hierarchically ranked in various ways. Employees are differentiated according to remuneration, job designation, clothing, degree of authority over others, and the degree to which they control their own work. A basic division is between the 'hourly paid' and those, such as foreman and above, who receive salaries. Nevertheless, it is still women who are portrayed as socially competitive, although in fact it is men who control the organization of production in our society.

A national survey of New Zealand's class structure in 1984 showed men to be over-represented in positions of economic power and control. They are more than twice as likely to be managers as women. In contrast, women, like Polynesians, are concentrated in the working class and very few control capital or productive property (Wilkes *et al.,* 1984: 18-21). Thus, economic inequalities, which profoundly affect the lives of both sexes, are predominantly controlled by men. This is sharply exposed in towns dominated by a single industry such as Kawerau and Tokoroa. Individuals find their everyday experiences — their access to employment, to income, to housing, their family's status position, and even the organization of domestic life — largely determined by the industry and its management (Chapple, 1976; James, 1987). The division between public production and the private sphere of the home, along with the interconnections between them, are starkly revealed in these towns, but they are equally significant elsewhere in New Zealand.

The division of labour between the sexes does not merely locate men in production and women in the home. It also allocates to women the task of policing the boundaries of class relations. Women are the instruments through which the relations of production are transformed into, and become indivisible from, the organization of class and status. Women's activities in maintaining class and status boundaries occur within structures imposed directly from the sphere of production. Occupational stratification within and between companies determines many expressions of status: housing, neighbourhood, friendships, and associations. As two tradesmen's wives in Kawerau explained, friendships or associations cutting across the mill's own hierarchies of work were frowned upon as disruptive of relations of authority, both within the mill and in the community as a whole:

Speaker 1 — You don't associate with your boss's wife that much. Or if it is, it's in a very subservient role.
Speaker 2 — Because if you do, hubby's friend will say 'what's he doing greasing up?'
Speaker 1 — The system is really stuffed up when hubby's on the paper machine and you're working on the [salaried] staff and mixing with the bosses.

While men's interests and institutional controls provide the parameters of women's status-seeking activities, men distance themselves in public situations from such activities. In public it is women, as wives and mothers with responsibilities for managing social contacts, who make sure that status divisions are maintained. However, ultimately, it is men's interests which direct women's activities in this arena:

We were the snobs. . . It was only because Dad never let us go out. My sister, she was the eldest, she was eighteen, and if she ever wanted to go out to a dance my mother had to go with her, and to make sure that she came home at the right time. Dad wasn't having his daughters lying around the streets and getting picked up by anything and anybody.

Clearly, while class and status distinctions are regarded as inappropriate in male mateship, men are certainly concerned with these matters when it comes to male-female mating.

Women's familial position as moral guardians and socializers imposes a burden of creating, maintaining, and passing on to the next generation the appropriate cultural capital (Bourdieu, 1979). It is women who ensure that their children acquire the appropriate styles, manners and presentation. They also ensure that this cultural capital is used to its best advantage by regulating their children's circle of friends, who are also potential marriage partners, by encouraging their school performance, by determining everyday patterns of consumption, and maintaining the friendship networks which are important to their husband's careers.

The 1984 national study of class in New Zealand shows that women have strong pro-capitalist attitudes. In every class their attitudes are stronger than men's attitudes and they are especially strong in the bourgeoisie; that is, the propertied[5] or capitalist class (Chrisp, 1986: 140-1). This suggests the considerable preoccupation of women with enhancing their family's position and opportunities, not only materially, but also in terms of prestige. Women in privileged positions of class are particularly concerned with ensuring their children's entry to élite schools and managing their social contacts in other ways, but less privileged women too 'want the best' for their children and strive for their upward social mobility, by emphasizing the value of an education (James, 1985: 200-3). Women are also frequently used by men to reflect their own success to their male colleagues and associates. As one of *The Smith Women* said:

He's Master at the Masonic Lodge, and it is a special year for them. That's involved me quite a bit. It's been a good excuse to buy more clothes! I've spent more on clothes this year than all my married life. (Barrington & Gray, 1981: 83.)

Men are distanced from implication in reproducing the class system because many class and status differences are seen to be artificially imposed on them through the machinations of a natural femininity. The identification of class and status distinctions with women helps to obscure real social and economic divisions. It is, thus, consonant with the view of New Zealand as an egalitarian society where it is believed there is ample opportunity for upward social mobility.

Since women appear to look after matters of class and status, men can afford to maintain 'a superficial "good fellowship" with others from a wide range of class and status positions' (James, 1979: 38). Indeed, for professional and bourgeois men, this is central to their ability to obtain information and contacts with colleagues and clients, and to maintain authority over employees. Such strategies are crucial to men's ability to reproduce and legitimate their positions of class. A Kawerau woman recalls:

John Spencer[6] [the owner] would walk through the mill. . . he'd walk up to [my husband] and chat, and, ask after me and the kids. . . here was this guy with all these pots of dough who wasn't the least bit, you know, snobbish.

Of course, not all the overt signs of inequality associated with race and class can be explained away as recourse to a 'natural' gender distinction. They need to be explained in other ways. Inequalities between men which cannot be ignored are reduced to differences in natural ability. Sport is especially important in this regard because, alongside the fostering of team spirit, it rewards individual ability. At the same moment, these differences do not threaten the ethos of egalitarianism because sporting ability does not overtly involve social inequalities. Sport and sporting figures are essential to male culture precisely because they epitomize non-threatening inequalities between men. They are non-threatening because their achievements can be rationalized as due to personal qualities and aptitudes innate to the individual rather than created by purposeful human action.

Sporting skills are seen to epitomize differences created by nature, not differences created by civilization. In the world of private business, the connection between sporting prowess and economic prowess constitutes a powerful symbol. Firstly, it appeals to notions of strength, daring, and aggressiveness which are embodied in sporting activities and are also seen as desirable in the business world (Gooding, 1987). Secondly, the symbolic connection between sport and economic power works to protect and legitimate the economic dominance of corporate bodies. Just as sporting ability is seen as natural, economic power and status are, by association, portrayed as natural and immutable qualities. It is not coincidental that the economically powerful in New Zealand frequently associate themselves with sporting pursuits. Corporate leaders have legitimized their economic dominance by co-opting sporting ventures. KZ7's entry into the America's Cup is merely one example.

The associations between the economic world, sport, and the 'national effort' cement alliances among men. Despite the inequalities experienced by working-class and Polynesian men, relative to bourgeois men, they nevertheless have an affinity, derived from male culture, from which women are excluded. This affinity is defined as natural. It underpins the mutual support that men, who in other situations may have quite opposing material interests, give to one another to maintain authority over women.

Maintaining Sex Inequalities

Ashley: Women's vision of the world shrinks til it is focused entirely on the family and its needs and cares. Men are still regarded as the primary breadwinners . . . I'm quite happy to care for the children at weekends, even change nappies, but it isn't my chief role. (Gray, 1983: 155.)

Norman: With the country the way it is and many woman working, it creates so many hassles. . . Harmony within the family will never be a reality again. . . Delinquency will remain until we get a 40-hour week and a wage that a couple can live on. (Gray, 1983: 138.)

Barbara: Well, you're just made to feel the inferior object of the partnership, I mean, this is my husband's upbringing. You're there to iron the shirts and cook the meals, and what have you. (James, 1985: 100.)

Fay: Men and women are different. If they weren't opposites there wouldn't be an attraction. (James 1985: 100.)

The gendered culture maintains sex inequalities by its emphasis on difference rather than on exclusion. As we have consistently argued, and demonstrated by the quotations above, the gendered culture associates different qualities and characteristics with each sex. Difference, then, is considered to be deeply and immutably rooted in biology. The different experiences of women and men are rarely portrayed as unequal. Instead women and men are seen as interdependent and complementary. The gendered culture conceals the degree to which material inequality between men and women exists in New Zealand.

The extent of these inequalities, as represented by women's access to social and economic resources, has been detailed in previous chapters and in other literature (Novitz, 1987b). Less obvious are the rewards women derive from a gendered culture and the benefits other interests derive from women's subordination. For women, the gendered culture portrays the private sphere of home and their tasks of wife and mother as autonomous. Neither men, nor employers, nor the State are seen as having rights to intervene in the areas of women's expertise. For many women, then, the home appears to be the only social space in which they can run their own lives. Women often respond by describing the benefits that they derive from their gender role. One Kawerau housewife asserted:

I can work my working day around my own timetable. I can do as I like, and when I like, and how I like it. If I want to live in a pigsty that's my prerogative. . . But a man has to do what his employer asks of him and expects of him. (James, 1985: 171-2.)

Certainly, women have much invested in accepting their primary involvement in the private sphere. As providers of services for loved ones, they obtain a sense of personal worth, social esteem, a certain financial and emotional security, and some interpersonal power. However, the irony is that the family life of the woman quoted above, and many like her, are largely governed by the routines of her husband's occupation. Women must have meals ready 'on call' for the male worker and must even sometimes fit their housework around the husband's working and sleeping schedules:

Women's domestic work is not only necessary and useful in the way it provides the backstage support for public life; it is also personally beneficial for a man to have a wife. (James, 1987: 107.)

Of course, men do exchange material support for women's work in the household and women's sexual and emotional services. However, this is hardly an equal exchange. For while men can replace women's services with those bought on the free market, women find it difficult to gain access to the disposable income necessary to buy such services or achieve rewards on the labour market comparable to men. Moreover, for men, women's primary identification with the home and their own assumed position as breadwinners can be used to support higher male remuneration in the workplace. For women, on the other hand, the assumption that they are not primarily income earners depresses their earning power.

The State encourages this association of women with unpaid labour. State policies not only assume that married women are non-earners, but, more significantly, that the responsibility for women's standard of living lies with husbands. Thus, the gendered culture in which the division of labour between the sexes and dependency are embedded, provides the means by which the State may eschew burdens imposed by its own commitment to welfare and to maintaining the incomes of all its citizens. Despite the over-representation of women among welfare beneficiaries, the State tends only to direct monies to these women because they are expected to be dependent (Saville-Smith, 1987a).

The State also reinforces women's identification with secondary earning by its consistent refusal to develop a public childcare system. The lack of either a comprehensive public or private childcare system indicates the extent to which women's domestic labour is exploited. Childcare undertaken by women in the home is considerably cheaper to taxpayers (predominantly men and companies) and to employers who are saved the expense of providing appropriate childcare facilities. The lack of childcare services has such a severe impact on women's labour market opportunities that paid work is frequently unattractive to many women. This leaves them vulnerable to exploitation as voluntary workers. In addition to their work within the home, women's unpaid labour is exploited by a variety of public and private agencies. These range from sports teams and community welfare organizations, to public companies who use their executives' wives' labour to organize the social environments in which rapport between businessmen can be established (James, 1979). Women's identification with unpaid labour makes them vulnerable to exploitation in the paid labour market. Women's responsibilities in the home, and their consequent need for flexible paid working hours, are used by employers to maximize labour output and to lower their overhead costs. Glide-time, part-time work, and piece work, which could be constructively used to make the labour market more responsive to all employees, have been used by employers to impose extremely low rates of pay on women. Novitz (1987b: 43) notes that in:

... 1984 some women outworkers reported working for about 50 cents an hour before tax. In contrast, one of the 'best firms in town' was reported to pay nearly $6 for one and a quarter hour's work.

Even the 'best firms' were paying considerably under the average hourly rate of around $7.70 in 1984 (Department of Statistics, 1987: 362). Just as racism becomes integral to the exploitation of Polynesian workers, so sexism, rationalized within the gendered culture, serves the interest employers have in maintaining a group of easily manipulated workers.

Conclusion

The gendered culture in New Zealand involves costs which fall on all of us to a greater or lesser extent, simply because its worst manifestations require intervention by the State or by other agencies. Despite such costs, the gendered culture is also intimately tied to maintaining inequalities of sex, race, and class to the benefit of men, those who own and control capital and other productive property, and Pākehā. Consequently, groups of people who often have immediately quite opposing interests may also have common interests.

Working-class men may have an interest in the exploitation of women's labour. This exploitation may be facilitated by a gendered culture, but it should not be forgotten that this same culture is a means by which men's own labour is exploited and their activism controlled. Similarly, while many feminists would like to regard gender as being an issue primarily to do with sex inequality and men's exploitation of women, we have seen that our gendered culture is a response to conflicts between employers and workers, Pākehā and Māori, as well as between men and women. It is dangerous, too, for advocates of Māori sovereignty to reject the problem of New Zealand's gendered culture as being only relevant to white women and men. It is true that Pākehā of all class positions and of both sexes derive benefits from the exclusion of the Māori. It is equally true that the gendered culture, and especially male culture, has been used as a means by which Māori, and Māori men in particular, have themselves gained benefits from accepting Pākehā domination. The gendered culture, then, provides not only a material *connection* between the dispossessed but a common material *interest*.

This is not to suggest that the cleavages between those at the bottom of the hierarchies of race, class, and sex are insignificant or unimportant. But it does suggest that at certain times, under certain conditions and in certain arenas, there is a potential, indeed a necessity, for the development of collective strategies which will allow each group to become politically, socially, and economically empowered. Polynesians, working-class men and women have, despite the exploitation, inequalities, and exclusions which occur among them, a real interest in building an equal society for they all bear the burden of inequality.

1 'Polynesian' includes Pacific Island Polynesian and Māori. The racism experienced by Pacific Islanders in New Zealand partly reflects their position as a migrant population, drawn to New Zealand to fill unskilled positions in the labour force since the Second World War. Inequalities of race, then, are structured differently for Māori and Pacific Islanders, because of differences between the positions of indigenous and migrant groups. However, they do share some common experiences. The experiences of Pacific Islanders also reflect the institutionalized racism which has been constructed out of the systematic exclusion of the Māori from social, political, and economic resources in our society since colonization. When the particular expression of racism affects Māori and Pacific Islander similarly, we refer to them together as Polynesian. Occasionally this combination is forced on us, even if not appropriate, because some statistics make no distinction between Māori and Pacific Islander.

2 An ethnic group is a group of people who share a common language, customs, religion, and ways of life. This is a cultural grouping. It is distinguished from a racial group. Racial categorization differentiates individuals simply on the basis of physical, visible difference, most notably colour (note Spoonley's (1988: 2-6, 40-4) extensive discussion of the development of these concepts).

Our major concern is with the divisions and inequalities between races in New Zealand. Māori and the various Pacific Island groups are distinct ethnically, but they often experience exclusion, not in the first instance on cultural grounds, but merely on the basis of colour.

3 Status is founded on differentiations expressed in consumption of such items as housing, education, goods, and services. It is a manifestation of the rewards which accrue to those in particular positions within the relations of production; that is, the ownership or lack of ownership of productive property such as capital, land, and assets.

4 The following quotes in this chapter which are not acknowledged are taken from fieldwork for the D.Phil. thesis of B. James, 1985.

5 Property in this sense refers to productive property such as capital, land, and productive assets including factories, machinery, and any other asset which allows an individual to make profit through the exploitation of someone else's labour.

6 Spencer, the pulp and paper industrialist, was the richest individual in New Zealand in August 1987, when he had an estimated monetary worth of $675 million (*Personal Investment,* 1987: 31).

Contesting a Gendered Culture

If the gendered culture is so much part of our way of life, if male dominance appears to be inevitable, and masculinity valued above femininity, what hope can there be for change? Are we destined to maintain a system which not only creates increasingly costly social problems, but helps to exclude so many in our society from much of the wealth and many of the resources they help to create? There seems no reason why this should be so. The gendered culture is a social construction, not a biological one, and is, consequently, not inevitable. It is not founded on any innate abilities on the part of men to excel in business, sports, politics, or violence, nor of women to be naturally suited to caring, cooking, and cleaning. On the contrary, the gendered culture in New Zealand is the consequence of historical and social conditions. Its maintenance, through the control exerted by certain groups over social resources and thus the living conditions and opportunities of other groups, is a profoundly social achievement which can be challenged and changed. However, change must be brought about by the collective actions of individuals. Those actions must confront the structures and practices of the gendered culture in both public and private.

A challenge to our gendered culture most obviously entails abandoning the restrictive femininity prescribed by our gendered culture. But it also means redefining masculinity by promoting the alternative and subordinated masculinities which are not built on male dominance over women (Connell, 1987: 184-6) and male exclusivity. Because the gendered culture is experienced at the personal level by individuals actually 'taking on' femininity or masculinity, resistance must, in the first instance, be an individual responsibility. If the gendered culture is to be replaced by more equal social arrangements, there must be a personal commitment to its demise.

The Gendered Culture and Individual Action

The notion of individual responsibility may seem at odds with the tenor of our discussion. Hitherto, it has been consistently argued that structures of inequality embody relations of domination and subordination which, in turn, inform and constrain the experiences of individuals. Moreover, we have asserted that changing individual attitudes or values pertaining to such problems as domestic violence or alcohol abuse is insufficient and ultimately ineffective. (A focus on attitudes or values hides structural relations and consequently transforms social problems into a problem of individual moral character.) Nevertheless, the type of structural analysis that we have pursued does not absolve individuals from the responsibility of bringing about change. It simply recognizes that individuals live within existing social relations, the nature of which must be taken into account when devising strategies for change.

While the gendered culture maintains inequalities, it also provides a site in which those structures of inequalities are made vulnerable. In our society, few workers hold positions in which they can directly or effectively confront the economic operations of the bourgeoisie. Similarly, the Māori have, until the 1970s, been so completely pushed to the margins of New Zealand's social, political, and economic life that their plight has been relatively easy to ignore. Women too, generally lack the power to challenge the structures of inequality among the sexes. Who can women confront, for instance, in the struggle against impoverishment and their consequent social and physical vulnerability?

The lack of a clear arena in which the protagonists meet has made the challenges of oppressed groups too frequently unfocused, too easily co-opted, and too often defused. However, the gendered culture, which actually serves to ensure that there is no arena in which protagonists can directly confront each other, is within the ambit of individuals. Individuals in their daily life, in work and leisure, in families and outside them, with friends and colleagues, both actively and passively, maintain a gendered culture. This fact alone provides opportunities for individuals in personal ways to challenge the arrangements of social inequality.

Two major areas to be reorganized, if we are to undermine the gendered culture, are the running of the household and caring for others (Barrett and McIntosh, 1982: 140-59; Connell, 1987: 280-93). In both these, the expectations of a division of labour and economic inequalities between the sexes maintain structures of sexual subordination. The solution in theory is simple. Whereas in practice it brings major problems. Men primarily, but older children too, must do their share of housework and cooking. Men must take greater responsibility for childcare, and the care of other relatives and dependants within the community. These innovations require major changes to the relationships between adult partners and between adults and children. Some go so far as to say that in order for these to be successfully accomplished, the nuclear family should be abolished (Firestone, 1972). This is not our position. Rather than abolition, we suggest that we as a society must explore different family forms and social groups, and discover the ways in which they can support individuals.

The nuclear family is not the only environment in which children can be raised successfully and where adults obtain physical and emotional support. Increasingly, solo-parent households, despite inadequate State support, are providing for the material and emotional needs of their members. Others choose to develop lifestyles which include communal living, homosexuality, or freedom from child-rearing.

These alternative ways of structuring private life do not guarantee equality between the sexes. Indeed, they may perpetuate the gendered culture. So-called 'liberated' living arrangements and 'open' relationships often, in subtle ways, obscure the continued association of women with nurturance and domesticity. Nevertheless, they may open up new ways of providing for everyday needs. Similarly, the nuclear family does not necessarily have to operate along lines of male authority and female dependence. Those working for relationships based on equality of sex within this structure are contributing to undermining the gendered culture.

Inevitably, the practical problems in seeking to change male and female culture are immense. The most pressing problem, especially for those couples where the male partner is clearly the major income earner, is the economic survival of the household if he is to curtail his earning ability by greater domestic involvement. Bourgeois and middle-class couples may be able to organize the household's resources and other supports to ensure that the woman has the opportunity for career development. However, for working-class couples, the opportunities for either partner are few. Many of these families may already rely on the woman working in a low paid job to supplement the man's. Frequently, some women, because of increasing male unemployment, become the main income earner and their husbands' domestic worker. This is not always an innovative 'role reversal', but a necessary response to the exigencies of the labour market.

For the poor who must eke out a living with few material resources and, consequently, few options, the ability to initiate change is limited. Change, for these people, presents a prospect of social and economic disorder from which they can neither escape nor construct alternatives. People are prisoners of the material circumstances which prevent them from challenging well-established social arrangements. Nevertheless, if women as a group are ever to get out of the secondary and thus subordinated earner status, there must be a widespread reassessment of the relative importance of men's employment, as opposed to women's. This necessitates changes not just within the home, but also in the structure of work. In the workplace, policies concerning employment equity, sexual harassment, parental childcare leave, and childcare facilities are issues of particular concern for working-class women. Their conditions of employment and opportunities for training and career development lag behind those of middle-class women.

Public and private institutions constrain our actions, but within those constraints some people attempt to create what Connell (1987: 281) describes as 'liberated zones'. These can be physical spaces, in which less powerful groups can draw strength. For women, these include women's centres and refuges, and for Māori, the marae serves such a purpose. Liberated zones are also social spaces. They can be:

a particular institution or part of one, a network of relationships or simply a group of people, where a degree of sex equality has been achieved, heterosexism eliminated, or counter-sexist practice sustained. (Connell, 1987: 281.)

While the establishment of 'liberated zones' is not easy they remain one of the most attainable goals for individuals acting to change their everyday lives.

'Liberated zones' are those parts of social existence from which the unthinking rituals of the gendered culture are banished. Their creation involves individuals in critically identifying and assessing the rituals of everyday life in terms of their coercive and exploitative nature. Such rituals abound. In sport many men's cricket clubs rely on wives and girlfriends to attend the club rooms not only to make tea for the players but to clean up the dishes. Why does this continue when, after all, only two batsmen are on the field at any one time leaving at least nine able-bodied men to prepare drinks? Perhaps cricket and other sports teams could actually employ someone to provide such a service.

Of course, everyday rituals are maintained not only by those who demand service but also by those who provide it. The social pressure on wives and girlfriends by other women to join these 'support-teams' is frequently enormous, particularly when the opportunity to wash dishes is presented as a significant means by which to 'meet people' and make friends. The extent to which this attracts women is a telling reflection of women's continued social isolation and privatization.

The domestic work which women do in supporting many of men's leisure activities is analogous to the unpaid work women do within the household. There are significant differences, however, which make challenging the organization of the former easier than confronting the latter. Within the household many women are economically dependent on their male partners. There is a structured, if unequal, exchange within the household. Moreover, women's obligations to engage in unpaid domestic labour are bound up with strong affective feelings for family members. On the other hand, the domestic support women provide for male collective activities neither directly involves an economic dependency relationship nor emotional ties. (It is true, of course, that individual men may exploit these private relations with individual women to get them to provide support for the activities of his mates or colleagues in play.) Under these conditions, both women and men have greater choices about resisting or changing the rituals of a gendered culture. Women can refuse an exploitative use of their labour. Men can take more responsibility for the 'housekeeping' requirements of their leisure activities.

There are many spaces in which 'liberated zones' can be created, simply by refusing the routines and rituals of our gendered culture. There is no material compulsion to indulge in ritualistic drinking and driving, participating in drinking games is by choice, violent behaviour involves the decision to be violent. Men, who tend to be the perpetrators of these acts, must take the responsibility for them. They must create 'liberated zones', not merely for women, but for themselves, for they too have advantages to gain from destroying the gendered culture.

It is easy to place the blame on others for maintaining the rituals of a gendered culture. Many of us, men and women, prefer to distance ourselves by suggesting that we are mere onlookers. However, the audience too must resist, for rituals are primarily spectator oriented. By being a member of the audience, one becomes a participant. Women are often cast in such a role and become rather like the magician's lady-helper; a prop in the rituals of masculinity through ritualized feminine passivity and dependence. Whenever a sober woman is driven home after a social evening by a less than sober man, when women habitually and passively attend functions which they sincerely dislike 'for the sake of their husband', when they accept their own dependency and expect other women to do likewise, women become the perpetrators of a gendered culture. This endangers not only themselves but other women. It preserves the inequalities which divide our society.

To abolish the division of labour between the sexes in one's own household or to challenge it at the place of work, to question prevailing assumptions regarding masculinity and femininity, to reshape the pattern of leisure; in short, creating 'liberating zones', all help to undermine the gendered culture. There are limits of course. Already, as Novitz (1987b: 51) points out:

Many of us have developed individual strategies for combining paid and unpaid work that daily test our ingenuity and our energy... we try to accommodate demands on us as parents, and the children of our parents, as well as employees, husbands, wives, lovers and friends.

These demands often prove difficult to fulfil when they come into conflict with individual efforts to survive in the midst of the present allocation of tasks and rewards in our society.

Even for those who have, by virtue of their access to resources, the opportunity to reorganize the household's division of labour, it becomes an onerous exercise to challenge the gendered culture. Many institutions incorporate hierarchies of sex, class, and race, and most actively maintain the gendered culture. As we have seen, the gendered culture is so integral to our lives that it is simply unrealistic to expect individuals to undertake a perpetual crusade against it. Exhaustion, not social change, must be the consequence of such a strategy. Even if we could single-handedly conduct an assault on the gendered culture through our everyday lives, it would be ultimately ineffective. Individuals benefit from, or pay the costs of a gendered culture not as individuals, but as members of particular groups. It is a structural problem and must be challenged at the structural level by members or supporters of the groups who bear the burdens of the gendered culture.

Making Alliances in the Pursuit of an Equal Society

The strategies we have outlined so far are directed towards individuals challenging everyday behaviours in which traditional assumptions about masculinity and femininity are unthinkingly confirmed. However, these strategies do not simply challenge sex inequalities, nor should they be rejected merely as in the interests of women. It should be remembered that the gendered culture embodies and expresses more than sex inequalities.

The gendered culture in New Zealand did not only emerge from conflicting material interests between women and men. It arose out of a combination of crises. The Pākehā sought to enforce their power over Māori. The propertied or bourgeois class, under threat from the demands of the unpropertied and changing imperatives in the sphere of production, needed to reinforce their social, as well as economic, authority. The gendered culture, in short, grew out of the conditions under which Aotearoa was colonized by the British. From its early configuration in the late nineteenth century to the present day, the gendered culture has been as much about the inequalities of class and race as it has been about inequalities between men and women.

The gendered culture, precisely because it is a cultural response to the conflicts between interests embedded in hierarchies of class, race, and sex, provides an obvious site of attack and resistance for those with an interest in social equity. Unfortunately, activists with an interest in such a society have often been divided. Those involved in the struggles of the working class, the racially and the sexually oppressed, have tended to be rather wary of one another. Their relations have been reduced to either 'moral' support or, at worst, a mutual hostility aggravated by continual debates over whose oppression is most onerous, whose struggle is primary.[1] The concept of a gendered culture provides a way out of such impasses because it is clear that supporting a gendered culture, either actively or passively, contributes to, and may well exacerbate, the exploitations and exclusions faced by all.

The analysis of a gendered culture is a practical and political pursuit. It reveals why there are difficulties in creating and maintaining coalitions among the oppressed. They have contradictory interests in challenging the structures of inequality. Although they may be exploited through one particular system of inequality, they may also be involved in perpetuating other systems of inequality. By examining the gendered culture, those contradictions can be recognized and dealt with. By exposing the links between social problems, the inequalities of race, class, and sex, and the vested interests of élite groups, the notion of a gendered culture provides a space in which the disadvantaged and seemingly powerless may forge mutually empowering alliances.

Forming alliances does not necessarily involve the creation of formal organizational links between groups representing the interests of women, workers, and Māori. What it does require is effective working together. Especially important is the development of ways of communicating and the exchange of information. This involves careful consideration of the impact of the strategies one group might pursue on the interests of other groups. It also entails giving support to another group's aspirations even when they provide no apparent benefit to the pursuit of one's own goals. Above all, alliances demand the sorting out of the differences which separate the victims of exclusion based on reasons of race, sex, and class. This is not achieved by uncritical acceptance, but through constructive and imaginative debate. By their very nature, alliances challenge the determinism which insists that one can only speak if one has the personal experience of 'being a woman' or 'being a Māori' or 'being working class'. Of course, people should speak from their experience, but effective political action demands more than this. It demands that individuals 'do their homework', and find out about the circumstances of their own lives *in relation* to others (Gunew and Spivak, 1986: 139).

Pursuing Equality and the Role of the State

Alliances need to be directed towards some issue or object of concern. This will ultimately depend on the situation at any one time. However, there is one institution which, because of its pervasive influence on all aspects of social life, will always form the backdrop to political action. That institution is the State. Generally, the concern with the State will be issue-specific. That is, action will focus on particular laws, policies, and administrative processes set down by the State which regulate the various spheres of our social and economic life. At certain times, however, those pursuing a just society will have to confront the problem of the role of the State itself. The late 1980s is precisely such a moment, for while the State is directing a far-reaching programme of social and economic restructuring of the rest of our society, it is also being directed to restructure itself. This has a profound impact on the allocation of wealth, resources, and status in our society.

The State is popularly presented as primarily an administrative body designed to protect individual rights and freedoms and dedicated to ensuring the social and economic well-being of all its citizens (Titmuss, 1974). However, far from being a neutral entity, the State has strong conservative tendencies and frequently acts to maintain the social and economic power of dominant élite groups (George and Wilding, 1976; Gough, 1979; Simpson, 1984; Spoonley, 1988: 72-109).

The State in New Zealand has not only overseen the dispossession of the Māori from their lands, but has actively participated in it (Belich, 1986). Frequently the State has upheld the rights of the propertied against those of the unpropertied. Specific institutions within the State, such as the law, police, and the armed services, have all been mobilized by the State to protect capitalist interests (Simpson, 1984: 184-5). The State, too, has traditionally reinforced women's economic dependency on men and, by extension, their continued impoverishment (Saville-Smith, 1987a).

Nevertheless, the State cannot be dismissed as a mere extension of élite group interests. The State has a separate imperative; to maintain social order and to uphold its own legitimacy as promoter of the 'public good'. This makes any direct co-optation of the State by élite groups threatening to its very existence. The State may help to maintain the power of social and economic élites but it must also mitigate the negative effects thrown up by the exploitations perpetrated by those groups. Consequently at times, State policies contradict the immediate interests of élites and favour disadvantaged groups by redirecting, through welfare, resources to those who would be otherwise excluded from them. Over this century, the State has partially resolved the inherent tension between maintaining the power of élite groups and ensuring that social inequalities do not threaten social order. It has done this by mobilizing the gendered culture and establishing the parameters of male and female cultures in New Zealand.

The institutional position of the State which dictates its involvement in both maintaining and mitigating the inequalities of race, sex, and class, along with its singular connection to the gendered culture, makes the State an obvious site of concern for those seeking a just society. To influence the State is even more important when it is being threatened with dismantlement by those who have an interest, not in equality, but, rather, in inequality.

The Wealthy, the State, and the Politics of Selfishness

The State has never seriously attempted to redistribute wealth in New Zealand. But it has since the late 1890s virtually underwritten a basic standard of living for its citizens. Particularly since the 1930s, the State has employed income-maintenance strategies such as welfare payments, tax reliefs, and subsidies for families on low incomes (Castles, 1985). The State has also provided services such as public works, health, housing, education, the protection of persons and property, and full-employment policies in which the State itself participated by becoming a major employer. These services were funded through taxation and were available to all. In this way, some resources were transferred from those with high incomes and easy access to resources to the poor.

These policies of resource transfer were developed in the midst of struggle. Many were wrested from an unwilling State by disadvantaged groups or conceded under the threat of social disorder. For the wealthy, the large companies, owners of productive property, and affluent professionals and entrepreneurs, such policies pose an opportunity cost. The State through taxation takes monies which the affluent would prefer to control in their own individual interests. As Novitz (1987a: 5) points out, all these groups have an interest in minimizing personal taxation and supporting cut backs in State services. For them, social well-being involves the removal of the State from the regulation of social and economic life. The State's provision of resources and services may lead to a 'fairer society', but such policies are associated with, as Treasury points out, opportunity costs for certain individuals (Novitz, 1987a: 2). That is, it is more advantageous for the affluent to use their funds to buy services on the open market than to subsidize welfare programmes through personal taxation, despite the fact that they have access to and rely on State services. Out of these interests has emerged demands for the devolution of the State, demands which have been supported in the late 1980s by the Treasury and expressed in the development of New Zealand's monetarism popularly known as Rogernomics.

The model for State devolution pursued by those representing the interests of the propertied and newly affluent sections of the middle class is a consumer sovereignty model (Fougere, 1987). This model embodies an individualistic view of social relations in which social well-being is allegedly maintained by the:

> . . . private actions of individuals and people in voluntary social networks. The voluntary exchange of goods, the natural cohesion of families and the spontaneous growth of social organizations are all basic to our social well-being. (Treasury, 1987: 122.)

Advocates of consumer sovereignty argue that the devolution of State responsibilities by creating private, competing, and profit-making services in all spheres, including health and education, will empower the users of those systems. This is because users are supposedly provided with the opportunity to choose where to take their business. Those who favour this position also argue that such a system is efficient because individuals have the right to withdraw or invest their resources in the provision of goods and services wherever they feel they can get the best value for money. This position is epitomized by the Task Force on Health in its 'Discussion Document on Treatment Services'. In it, the authors state:

> If money was equitably available to consumers then the competitive market would provide the best solution just as it does for other necessities such as food, clothing, and housing. (Cited in de Jongh, 1987: 50.)

However, the reality is that the competitive market has proved to be an inefficient provider of these necessities. For instance, the 'free market' in housing has left an estimated 20,000 families homeless and a considerable number of single people without accommodation (Waldegrave and Coventry, 1987: 24). Why does the 'free market' fail? Because, in the real world, money is *not* available equitably.

Māori, working-class people, and women have relatively few income resources. Indeed, as Fougere (1987) has commented, it was precisely the failure of the consumer sovereignty model in the nineteenth and early twentieth centuries to provide for these people's needs which forced the State to assume, centralize, and institutionalize the provision of basic services. Unless other measures are imposed which ensure that each individual in our society has exactly the same income, consumer sovereignty will place the responsibility of health, education, and welfare on to the shoulders of individuals and groups, yet will fail to redistribute adequately resources necessary for individuals to undertake those responsibilities.

Ultimately, the situation of the affluent and the poor *vis-à-vis* the State is entirely different. For the affluent, the provision of services funded through taxation is an opportunity cost. For the poor, for those excluded from the ownership of productive property, and particularly those excluded from wage labour because of the dictates of profitability, age, illness, or commitments such as community and home care, there are few, if any, opportunity costs. Unless the State intervenes to provide goods and services, these people's incomes make their buying such services as individuals virtually impossible. Women and Polynesians persistently fall into these categories, male members of the working class frequently do. For those at the 'wrong' end of the hierarchies of race, class, and sex, social life is far from voluntary. Theirs is a world in which choice is a luxury and the notion of opportunity costs irrelevant. The affluent have a short-term interest in dismantling the State. But for women, Māori, and workers, the ability of the State to collect and consolidate resources and to provide services for public use is absolutely imperative.

Any dismantlement of the State through a consumer sovereignty model of devolution will increase inequalities in this society, directly and indirectly. Directly, the flow of resources to the under-resourced will be inhibited and their access to the basic necessities of housing, health care, and education will be even more limited. Indirectly, the devolution of the State advocated by supporters of consumer sovereignty will reinforce the gendered culture.

Devolution and the Gendered Culture

Devolution, as expressed by advocates of consumer sovereignty, does not ensure that local groups and consumers will have resources to fulfil their needs. It simply means that consumers will have the responsibility to service those needs. In under-resourced communities, devolution will rely on the exploitation of the largely voluntary work of community members. In the context of a society in which unpaid work is predominately done by women, the burdens of devolution will fall on women. This will undoubtedly exacerbate the cultural separation of women's 'world' from that of men's. The initial stages of devolution, found in the movement to 'community care', illustrates precisely this process.

Calls for the community to be more involved in the care of its members have frequently been presented as extending the range of choice to the individual regarding how, and by whom, they will be cared for. In reality, the history of community care has been marked by the tendency for communities to face greater responsibility rather than to receive the appropriate allocations of skills and resources needed to undertake those responsibilities. Under these conditions, community care projects such as Mātua Whāngai have relied on the unpaid labour of many, but particularly of women, as domestic workers and care-givers in the home, and as voluntary workers in the community (Ministerial Advisory Committee, 1986: 34).

Much of women's voluntary work deals with the care of dependants in the community such as the elderly, children, chronically ill, disabled, and handicapped (Horsfield, 1988: 295). In this context, community care actually means providing care within the home. Despite many women's willingness to undertake such work on what is usually a full-time basis, and their affection for the people for whom they provide care, these care-givers experience the burdens of isolation imposed by being virtually on call for twenty-four hours a day. Nevertheless, for many women, not to accept the role of carer is to 'face a frightening moral choice' (Society for Research on Women, 1976: 33) because of the seeming lack of alternative care structures on which they feel they can rely.

Apart from looking after family members, women have also been expected to care directly for the community. The backbone of voluntary work, women have been the innovators in fields such as the provision of support for sexually abused and beaten women, early childhood education and care, and community health initiatives. Yet there has typically been limited funding for such community development. This has had a profound impact on women, especially as the organizations which attempt to fulfil needs specific to women, such as Rape Crisis and groups aiding battered women, have had continual problems in attracting Government funding.

Because many of the immediate day-to-day burdens of hands-on care and of community development are shouldered by women, it is tempting to regard community care and State devolution as a women's problem or issue. However, it is much more than this. The expansion of women's unpaid work associated with community care means that the overall resources to which women, Māori, and Pākehā working-class men have access will be considerably reduced. These burdens are increasing precisely at the time when resources in communities are being threatened. It is no longer certain that women will be willing and able to take on further care. At the same time, fewer men are able to make a contribution to their community through paid work.

For working-class men as a whole, and Māori men especially, the security of employment has become increasingly problematical with the State's dismantlement of its full employment policy and its restructuring policies. Consequently, some categories of the population are expected to develop sophisticated forms of 'self-help' to substitute for centralized, State-administered services while the public resources which supported community care in the past are being eroded. Communities which are being hit by departmental restructuring and the loss of employment and services are, at the same time, being expected to provide community care.

By acquiescing to the continuing and indeed increased use of women's care to substitute for State services, we maintain the gendered culture and prevent the access of disadvantaged groups to social resources. If devolution is to be a strategy for greater equity, the assumptions currently determining its direction which focus on individualism and the market on the one hand, and the collective sacrifices of women as carers on the other, need to be overturned. To do so, the connection between the gendered culture and the delegation of State responsibility to 'the community' must be revealed and challenged.

Alternative Models for State Devolution

The full implications of State devolution have been obscured by the way in which the gendered culture works to fill the vacuum left by the discontinuation of State services. However, this is only one reason why the consumer sovereignty model of State devolution has been scarcely challenged by those who have an interest in a more just society. Another significant reason is that the Māori, unpropertied, and women experience real disadvantages from State intervention.

These groups may have received certain benefits from the State's redirection of resources through welfare, but in dispensing that welfare, the State bureaucracy has also intruded, insensitively and impersonally, into the running of everyday lives. Consumer sovereignty is alleged to provide consumers with choice on the market, but there is no evidence that it gives them power over resources. The type of devolution that the disadvantaged seek is more accurately expressed through the model of democratic sovereignty (Fougere, 1987).

Democratic sovereignty involves a set of partnerships between users and services which will allow resources to be developed in ways which fulfill users' understandings of their needs and efficiently mobilize the specialist knowledge and skills of service professionals. Democratic sovereignty is both a means by which individuals can be empowered and resources used efficiently. Such an approach recognizes that the vast majority of individuals in user-groups cannot afford to buy alternative goods and services on a privatized market directed solely by the pursuit of highest profits. It is an approach that acknowledges that only through collectivizing their monies with the monies of others can these individuals gain access to the resources necessary to provide adequate standards of health, education, and housing.

Conclusion

The gendered culture must be a primary target for those committed to building a more equitable society, for it is the structure in which the inequalities of class, race, and sex flourish. What we have attempted to provide is an analysis of the gendered culture which will allow people to examine their own conditions of existence and develop tactics to deal with them. Tactics for change fall into three broad categories: those which centre on individuals; those which centre on making and mobilizing links between those interested in a fairer society; and actions which focus on the State, its role, policies, and administrative practices.

Ultimately each of us has to decide to what extent we are committed to a just society and to what extent we really do want to deal with the problems of social order such as public and private violence or alcohol abuse. We as individuals, too, must decide, given the undoubted constraints on our lives, how many of these categories of action we feel able to pursue. All are important. Whatever choices we make, however, one thing is clear. We all, whether we are among the disadvantaged or among the privileged, bear some of the costs of the gendered culture. The social disruption which emerges from it is felt by all.

For those who by birth happen to be propertied and male and Pākehā, the benefits of a gendered culture may appear to outweigh the disadvantages, but even a Pākehā bourgeois man can be the victim of drinking and driving rituals. Moreover, the numbers of people in this society who fall into all three of these positions is very small. The vast majority of us have a real material interest in the re-creation of our culture because we are either Māori, or unpropertied, or women. It is for us to recognize that the direct, personal costs of the gendered culture far outweigh any benefits we might gain from it. It is time we grasped our common interest in the creation of new forms of masculinity and femininity.

1 See the preface for a brief account of the primacy debate. See also Awatere's (1984) discussion on alliances.

Resources

The following list is selective and incomplete, but should provide a variety of opportunities to obtain further information. These include:

(i) *Broadsheet* (PO Box 68026, Newton, Auckland). New Zealand's feminist magazine which carries news, articles, reviews, information on the feminist movement, and a regular directory of women's groups and organizations throughout New Zealand.

(ii) *Race, Gender, Class* (PO Box 1372, Christchurch). A journal which analyses inequalities in New Zealand.

(iii) *Women's Studies. A New Zealand Handbook* by C. Craven, *et al.* (New Women's Press, Auckland, 1985). This is a useful source of information, facts and figures, and suggestions for running women's studies courses. It also includes resources, lists of publications, videos, films, etc.

(iv) *Women's Studies Association* (PO Box 5067, Auckland) is a feminist organization which seeks to promote research and education. The organization, which has branches throughout New Zealand, holds yearly conferences and produces a journal.

(v) *Society for Research on Women* (PO Box 12-270, Wellington North) has published a range of research reports on women's issues.

(vi) *The Ministry of Women's Affairs* (Private Bag, Wellington) puts out a regular newsletter/Pānui which provides information on the Ministry's activities and publications. The Ministry also has a resource library.

(vii) *The Human Rights Commission* (PO Box 5045, Wellington) has many resources available, including the Sexual Harrassment Information Kit, videos, cassette tapes, and publications.

(viii) Finally, many areas have a variety of groups, such as Rape Crisis Centres, Women's Refuges, Battered Women's Groups, Women's Health Centres, Men Against Violence, and Worker's Educational Associations. To find out more about these organizations, ring your local Citizen's Advice Bureau.

Bibliography

Appendix to the Journals of the House of Representatives, 1890. 'Sweating Commission' H-5.

Asher, G., and Naulls, D., 1987. *Maori Land,* Wellington, New Zealand Planning Council.

Awatere, D., 1984. *Maori Sovereignty,* Auckland, Broadsheet Publications.

Bailey, J. 1986. *Towards the Extinction of the Drinking Driver in New Zealand: A Progress Report,* Wellington, Department of Scientific and Industrial Research.

Bailey, J., and Allo, D., 1987. *Convicted Drinking Drivers in Wellington Area 1987,* Wellington, Department of Scientific and Industrial Research.

Ball, M., 1986. *Footrot Flats. The Dog's Tail Tale*, Lower Hutt, Inprint Ltd.

Ballara, A., 1986. *Proud to be White?*, Auckland, Heinemann.

Barrett, M., 1980. *Women's Oppression Today. Problems in Marxist Feminist Analysis*, London, Verso.

Barrett, M., and McIntosh, M., 1982. *The Anti-Social Family*, London, Verso.

Barrington, R., and Gray, A., 1981. *The Smith Women*, Wellington, A.H. and A.W. Reed.

Bedggood, D., 1980. *Rich and Poor in New Zealand: A Critique of Class, Politics and Ideology*, Auckland, Allen and Unwin.

Bell, C., and Adair, V., 1985. *Women and Change. A Study of New Zealand Women*, Wellington, National Council of Women.

Belich, J., 1986. *The New Zealand Wars and the Victorian Interpretation of Racial Conflict*, Auckland, Auckland University Press.

Best, E., 1974. *The Maori as He Was: A brief account of Maori life as it was in pre-European days*, Wellington, A.R. Shearer, Government Printer.

Binney, J., and Chaplin, G., 1986. *Nga Morehu. The Survivors*, Auckland, Oxford University Press.

Bourne, J., 1984. 'Towards an Anti-Racist Feminism', *Race and Class*, Pamphlet No. 9.

Bourdieu, P., 1979. *Distinction. A Social Critique of the Judgement of Taste*, London, Routledge and Kegan Paul.

Bradbury, J., 1984. *Violent Offending and Drinking Patterns*, Wellington, Institute of Criminology, Victoria University.

Brittan, A., and Maynard, M., 1984. *Sexism, Racism and Oppression*, Oxford, Basil Blackwell.

Broadsheet, 1985. 'Forum Fever', January/February: 12-18.

Brooking, T., 1984. 'Economic Transformation', pp. 226-49 in W. Oliver (ed), *The Oxford History of New Zealand*, Wellington, Oxford University Press.

Bunkle, P., 1980. 'The Origins of the Women's Movement in New Zealand: The Women's Christian Temperance Union 1885-1895', pp. 52-76 in P. Bunkle and B. Hughes (eds), *Women in New Zealand Society*, Sydney, Allen and Unwin.

Butterworth, S., 1974. 'Autres Temps, Autres Moeurs', *New Zealand Listener*, March 30:14.

Calvert, S., 1978. *Women in Mental Health in New Zealand*, Hamilton, Occasional Working Paper of the Women's Studies Association, No. 1.

Castles, F., 1985. *The Working Class and Welfare*, Wellington, Allen and Unwin/Port Nicholson Press.

Caswell, S., 1980. *Drinking by New Zealanders*, Auckland, Alcohol Research Unit, University of Auckland, and Alcoholic Liquor Advisory Council.

Chapple, D., 1976. *Tokoroa: Creating a Community*, Auckland, Longman Paul.

Chaytor, M., 1980. 'Household and Kinship: Ryton in the late sixteenth and early seventeenth centuries', *History Workshop Journal*, 10:25-60.

Chrisp, P., 1986. 'Class of '84: Class Structure and Class Awareness in New Zealand, 1984', M.A. Thesis, Department of Sociology, Massey University, Palmerston North.

Coney, S., 1981. 'Women Against the Tour', *Broadsheet*, September: 8-11.

Coney, S., 1986. 'The Heavy Expense of Being Male', *New Zealand Sunday Times*, 26 October.

Connell, R.W., 1983. *Which Way is Up: Essays on Class, Sex and Culture*, Sydney, Allen and Unwin.

Connell, R.W., 1987. *Gender and Power,* Sydney, Allen and Unwin.

Coughlan, K., 1987. '"Good Kiwi Girls" Behind The Good Kiwi Yachts', *Dominion Sunday Times,* 28 July.

Cox, S., and James, B., 1987. 'The Theoretical Background', pp. 1-22 in S. Cox (ed), *Public and Private Worlds: Women in Contemporary New Zealand,* Wellington, Allen & Unwin/Port Nicholson Press.

Craig, T., and Mills, M., 1987. *Care and Control. The Role of Institutions in New Zealand,* Social Monitoring Group Report No. 2, New Zealand Planning Council, Wellington.

Dalziel, R., 1986. 'The Colonial Helpmeet. Women's Role and the Vote in Nineteenth-Century New Zealand', pp. 55-68 in B. Brookes *et al.* (eds), *Women in History. Essays on European Women in New Zealand,* Wellington, Allen and Unwin/Port Nicholson Press.

Dann, C., 1982. 'The Game is Over', *Broadsheet,* March: 26-8.

Dann, C., 1985. *Up from Under. Women and Liberation in New Zealand 1970-1985,* Wellington, Allen & Unwin.

David, D., and Brannon, R., 1976. *The Forty-Nine Percent Majority; The Male Sex Role,* Massachusetts, Addison-Wesley Publishing Co.

Davis, A., 1982. *Women Race and Class,* London, The Women's Press.

Dean, M., 1979. 'Battered Wives', *Women's Studies Association Newsletter,* 5: 4-21.

de Jong, P., 1986. '"Looking Forward to Saturday": A Social History of Rugby in a Small New Zealand Township', M.A. Thesis, Department of Sociology, Massey University, Palmerston North.

de Jong, P., 1987. 'The Old Rugby Grows on You', *Sites,* 14 (Autumn): 35-56.

de Jongh, R., 1987. 'Healthy, Wealthy or Die', *New Zealand Listener,* 19 December: 50-1.

Department of Statistics, 1984a. *New Zealand Official Yearbook 1984,* Wellington, Government Printer.

Department of Statistics, 1984b. *Justice Statistics, Part B,* Wellington, Government Printer.

Department of Statistics, 1986. *New Zealand Official Yearbook 1985,* Wellington, Government Printer.

Department of Statistics, 1987. *New Zealand Official Yearbook 1986-87,* Wellington, Government Printer.

Donnelly, F., 1978. *Big Boys Don't Cry,* Auckland, Cassell.

Donzelot, J., 1979. *The Policing of Families,* New York, Pantheon Books.

Eldred-Grigg, S., 1977. 'Whatever Happened to the Gentry? The Large Landowners of Ashburton County, 1890-1896', *New Zealand Journal of History,* 11 (1): 3-27.

Eldred-Grigg, S., 1984. *Pleasures of the Flesh, Sex and Drugs in Colonial New Zealand 1840-1915,* Wellington, A.H. and A.W. Reed Ltd.

Evison, H., 1986. *Ngai Tahu Land Rights and the Crown Pastoral Lease Lands in the South Island of New Zealand,* Christchurch, Ngai Tahu Maori Trust Board.

Fairburn, M., 1979. 'Social Mobility and Opportunity in Nineteenth-Century New Zealand', *New Zealand Journal of History,* 13 (1): 43-60.

Fairburn, M., 1985. 'Vagrants, "Folk Devils" and Nineteenth-Century New Zealand as a Bondless Society', *Historical Studies,* 21 (85): 495-514.

Fergusson, D., *et al.,* 1979. 'Factors Association With Ex-Nuptial Birth', *New Zealand Medical Journal,* 89 (633): 248-50.

Firestone, S., 1972. *The Dialectic of Sex,* London, Paladin.

Firth, R., 1973. *Economics of the New Zealand Maori,* Wellington, Government

Printer.

Fletcher, G., 1978. 'Division of Labour in the New Zealand Nuclear Family', *New Zealand Psychologist*, 7 (2): 33-40.

Ford, G., 1986. *Research Project on Domestic Disputes: Final Report*, Wellington, Police National Headquarters.

Fougere, G., 1981. 'Barbed Wire and Riot Squads — What is Being Defended?', *New Zealand Cultural Studies Working Group Newsletter*, 2: 2-5.

Fougere, G., 1987. 'Devolution and Health Systems', *New Zealand Sociological Association Conference Proceedings*, Palmerston North, Massey University.

Furbank, P., 1985. *Unholy Pleasure: The Idea of Social Class*, Oxford, Oxford University Press.

Gallie, D., 1983. *Social Inequality and Class Radicalism in France and Britain*, Cambridge, Cambridge University Press.

Gardner, W., 1984. 'A Colonial Economy', pp. 57-86 in W. Oliver (ed), *The Oxford History of New Zealand*, Wellington, Oxford University Press.

George, V., and Wilding, P., 1976. *Ideology and Social Welfare*, London, Routledge and Kegan Paul.

Gluckman, L.K., 1976. *Tangiwai. A Medical History of Nineteenth Century New Zealand*, Christchurch, Whitcoulls.

Gooding, B., 1987. *KZ7. Inside Stories of Fear and Loathing*, Auckland, Reed Methuen.

Gough, I., 1979. *The Political Economy of the Welfare State*, London, Macmillan.

Graham, J., 1984. 'Settler Society', pp. 140-67 in W. Oliver (ed), *The Oxford History of New Zealand*, Wellington, Oxford University Press.

Grant, I., 1980. *The Unauthorised Version. A Cartoon History of New Zealand*, Auckland, Cassell.

Gray, A., 1983. *The Jones Men*, Wellington, A.H. and A.W. Reed.

Griffin, C., 1985. *Typical Girls: Young Women from School to the Job Market*, London, Routledge and Kegan Paul.

Gunew, S., and Spivak, G.C., 1986. 'Questions of Multiculturalism', *Hecate*, 12 (1/2): 136-42.

Hall, G., 1987. *Two-Income Families in New Zealand*, Research Series 6, Wellington, Research Section, Department of Social Welfare.

Hamer, D., 1965. 'Sir Robert Stout and the Labour Question, 1870-1893', pp. 78-101 in R. Chapman and K. Sinclair (eds), *Studies of a Small Democracy*, Auckland, Auckland University Press.

Hawke, G., 1985. *The Making of New Zealand. An Economic History*, Cambridge, Cambridge University Press.

Hodges, I., 1985. 'Drinking Vernacular and the Negotiation of Intimacy', *Sites* 11: 13-19.

Horsfield, A., 1988. *Women in the Economy*, Wellington, Ministry of Women's Affairs.

Horsfield, A., and Evans, M., 1988. *Maori Women in the Economy*, Wellington, Ministry of Women's Affairs.

Howe, K., 1977. *Race Relations: Australia and New Zealand: A Comparative Survey 1770s-1970s*, Wellington, Methuen.

Jackson, M., 1978. 'Battered Wives: Why do They Stay?', *Broadsheet*, November: 26-9.

James, B., 1982. 'Feminism: Making the Private World Public', pp. 232-50 in I. Shirley (ed), *Development Tracks. The Theory and Practise of Community Development*, Palmerston North, Dunmore Press.

James, B., 1985. 'Mill Wives. A Study of Gender Relations, Family and Work in a Single-Industry Town', D. Phil. Thesis, Department of Sociology, Waikato University, Hamilton.

James, B., 1986. 'A Great Place to Raise a Family? New Zealand Family Policy and the Welfare State', pp. 129-209 in C. Wilkes (ed), *Working Papers on the State,* Palmerston North, Department of Sociology, Massey University.

James, B., 1987. 'Millworkers Wives', pp. 103-23 in S. Cox (ed), *Public and Private Worlds: Women in Contemporary New Zealand,* Wellington, Allen and Unwin/Port Nicholson Press.

James, K., 1979. 'The Home: A Public or Private Place? Class, Status and the Actions of Women', *Australian and New Zealand Journal of Sociology,* 15 (1), 36-42.

Jesson, B., 1987. *Behind the Mirror Glass. The Growth of Wealth and Power in New Zealand in the Eighties,* Auckland, Penguin.

Jones, G., 1984. 'Working Class Culture and Working Class Politics in London, 1780-1900', *Journal of Social History,* 7: 460-507.

Kawharu, I.H., 1977. *Maori Land Tenure. Studies of a Changing Institution.* Oxford, Oxford University Press.

Kedgley, S., 1985. *The Sexual Wilderness: Men and Women In New Zealand,* Auckland, Reed Methuen.

King, M., 1983. *Maori. A Photographic and Social History,* Auckland, Heinemann.

King, M., 1984. 'Between Two Worlds', pp. 279-301 in W. Oliver (ed), *The Oxford History of New Zealand,* Wellington, Oxford University Press.

Koopman-Boyden, P., and Scott, C., 1984. *The Family and Government Policy in New Zealand,* Sydney, Allen and Unwin.

Lange, D., 1986. 'The New Welfare State', The Mackintosh Memorial Lecture, 9 June, Prestonpans, Scotland.

Leckie, J., 1985. 'In Defence of Race and Empire. The White New Zealand League at Pukekohe', *New Zealand Journal of History,* 19 (2): 103-29.

MacDonald, C., 1986. 'The "Social Evil"', pp. 13-34 in B. Brookes *et al.* (eds), *Women in History: Essays on European Women in New Zealand,* Wellington, Allen and Unwin/Port Nicholson Press.

McGeorge, C., 1981. 'Race and the Maori in the New Zealand Primary School Curriculum Since 1877', *ANZHES Journal,* 10 (1): 13-23.

McKinlay, P., 1987. *Corporatisation: The Solution for State Owned Enterprise?,* Wellington, Victoria University Press/Institute of Policy Studies.

McLaughlan, G., 1976. *The Passionless People,* Auckland, Cassell.

Mahuika, A., 1975. 'Leadership: Inherited and Achieved', pp. 86-114 in M. King (ed), *Te Ao Hurihuri. The World Moves On,* Wellington, Hicks Smith and Sons Ltd.

Makereti, 1986. *The Old-time Maori,* Auckland, New Women's Press.

Management Services and Research Unit, 1983. *Health Facts New Zealand,* Wellington, Department of Health.

Mataira, P., 1987. 'A Study of Alcohol Consumption on Maraes and of Contemporary Drinking Patterns in Ruatoria', M. Phil. Thesis, Department of Sociology, Massey University, Palmerston North.

Miller, J., 1974. *Early Victorian New Zealand. A Study of Racial Tension and Social Attitudes 1839-1852,* Wellington, Oxford University Press.

Mills, C.W., 1970. *The Sociological Imagination,* Harmondsworth, Penguin.

Ministerial Task Force on Income Maintenance, 1986. *Benefit Reform,* Wellington, Ministerial Task Force on Income Maintenance.

Ministerial Advisory Committee on a Maori Perspective for the Department of Social Welfare, 1986. *Puao-te-Ata-Tu (Daybreak)*, Wellington, Department of Social Welfare.

Ministerial Committee of Inquiry into Violence, 1987. *Report of the Ministerial Committee of Inquiry into Violence*, Wellington, Government Printer.

Murphy, Y., and Murphy R., 1985. *Women of the Forest*, Columbia University Press, New York.

National Health Statistics Centre, 1985. *Mortality and Demographic Data*, Wellington, Department of Health.

New Zealand Police, 1986. *Police Submissions to the Ministerial Committee of Inquiry into Violence*, Wellington, New Zealand Police.

Novitz, R., 1978. 'Marital and Familial Roles in New Zealand: The Challenge of the Women's Liberation Movement', pp. 71-86 in P. Koopman-Boyden (ed), *Families in New Zealand Society*, Wellington, Methuen.

Novitz, R., 1987a. 'Treasury: A Sociological Analysis', *New Zealand Sociological Association Conference Proceedings*, Palmerston North, Massey University.

Novitz, R., 1987b. 'Bridging the Gap: Paid and Unpaid Work', pp. 23-52 in S. Cox (ed), *Public and Private Worlds: Women in Contemporary New Zealand*, Wellington, Allen and Unwin/Port Nicholson Press.

Oakley, A., 1972. *Sex Gender and Society*, Bath, Pitman Press.

O'Connor, P., 1968. 'Keeping New Zealand White, 1908-1920', *New Zealand Journal of History*, 2 (1): 41-65.

Olssen, E., 1984. 'Towards a New Society' pp. 250-78 in W. Oliver (ed), *The Oxford History of New Zealand*, Wellington, Oxford University Press.

Olssen, E. 1977. 'Social Class in Nineteenth Century New Zealand', pp. 22-41 in D. Pitt (ed), *Social Class in New Zealand*, Auckland, Longman Paul.

Olssen, E., 1980. 'Women, Work and Family 1880-1926', pp. 159-83 in P. Bunkle and B. Hughes (eds), *Women in New Zealand Society*, Sydney, Allen and Unwin.

Olssen, E., and Levesque, A., 1978. 'Towards a History of the European Family in New Zealand', pp. 1-26 in P. Koopman-Boyden (ed), *Families in New Zealand Society*, Wellington, Methuen.

Oxley, H. 1978. *Mateship in Local Organisation*, St Lucia, University of Queensland Press.

Pahl, R., 1984. *Divisions of Labour*, Oxford, Basil Blackwell.

Park, J., 1985. *Towards an Ethnography of Alcohol in New Zealand*, Auckland, Department of Anthropology, University of Auckland.

Parkin, F., 1979. *Marxism and Class Theory: a bourgeois critique*, London, Tavistock.

Pearson, D., and Thorns, D., 1983. *Eclipse of Equality*, Wellington, Allen & Unwin.

Pere, R., 1982. *Ako, Concepts and Learning in the Maori Tradition*, Working Paper No. 17, Department of Sociology, Waikato University, Hamilton.

Personal Investment, 1987. 'The Rich 100', August: 27-61.

Phillips, J., 1980. 'Mummy's Boys: Pakeha Men and Male Culture in New Zealand', pp. 217-43 in P. Bunkle and B. Hughs (eds), *Women in New Zealand Society*, Sydney, Allen and Unwin.

Phillips, J., 1987. *A Man's Country? The Image of the Pakeha Male: A History*, Auckland, Penguin.

Phillips, R., 1981. *Divorce in New Zealand: A Social History*, Auckland, Oxford University Press.

Pow, G., 1986. *The Psychological consequences of Sexual Assault: A Literature Review*, Research Report no. 102, Wellington, Accident Compensation Corporation.

Pratt, J., 1987. 'Law and Order Politics in New Zealand 1986: A Comparison with the United Kingdom 1974-9', Unpublished paper, Department of Social

Policy and Social Work, Massey University, Palmerston North.

Rangihau, J., 1975. 'Being Maori', pp. 221-33 in M. King (ed), *Te Ao Hurihuri. The World Moves On.* Wellington, Hicks Smith and Son Ltd.

Rayner T., Chetwynd, J., and Alexander, T., 1984. *Costs of Alcohol Abuse in New Zealand. A Premilinary Investigation,* Wellington, Alcoholic Liquor Advisory Council.

Reiger, K., 1985. *The Disenchantment of the Home. Modernizing the Australian Family 1880-1940,* Melbourne, Oxford University Press.

Richardson, L., 1984. 'Parties and Political Change', pp. 197-225 in W. Oliver (ed), *The Oxford History of New Zealand,* Wellington, Oxford University Press.

Ritchie, J., and Ritchie J., 1978. *Growing Up in New Zealand,* Sydney, Allen and Unwin.

Rosaldo, M., 1980. 'The Use and Abuse of Anthropology: Reflections on Feminism and Cross-Cultural Understanding', *Signs,* 5(3): 389-417.

Ryan, A., 1986. ' "For God, Country and Family": Populist Moralism and the New Zealand Moral Right', *New Zealand Sociology,* 1(2): 104-12.

Salmond, A., 1976. *Hui: A Study of Maori Ceremonial Gatherings,* Auckland, Reed Methuen.

Saville-Smith, K., 1987a. 'Women and the State', pp. 193-210 in S. Cox (ed), *Public and Private Worlds: Women in Contemporary New Zealand,* Wellington, Allen and Unwin/Port Nicholson Press.

Saville-Smith, K., 1987b. 'Rape: The Social Construction of Rape Trauma and Social Control', Paper presented at the S.A.A.N.Z. Conference, Sydney, 14-17 July.

Saville-Smith, K., 1987c. 'Producing Reproduction: Rethinking Feminist Materialism', *New Zealand Sociology,* 2 (1): 51-62.

Scott, H., 1976. *Women and Socialism: Experiences from Eastern Europe,* London, Allison and Busby Ltd.

Segal, L., 1987. *Is the Future Female? Troubled Thoughts on Contemporary Feminism,* London, Virago.

Select Committee on Violent Offending, 1979. *Report of the Select Committee on Violent Offending,* Wellington, Government Printer.

Simpson, T., 1979. *Te Riri Pakeha. The White Man's Anger,* Auckland, Hodder and Stoughton.

Simpson, T., 1984. *A Vision Betrayed. The Decline of Democracy in New Zealand,* Auckland, Hodder and Stoughton.

Sinclair, D., 1975. 'Land: Maori View and European Response', pp. 115-40 in M. King (ed), *Te Ao Hurihuri. The World Moves On,* Wellington, Hicks Smith and Sons Ltd.

Sinclair, K., 1986. *A Destiny Apart. New Zealand's Search for National Identity,* Wellington, Allen & Unwin/Port Nicholson Press.

Smith, P. 1985. 'Rugby Finds Itself on WAR Footing', *New Zealand Sunday Times,* 28 April.

Social Advisory Council, 1987. *Meeting the Needs of Families,* Wellington, Social Advisory Council.

Society for Research on Women, 1976. *Those Who Care,* Wellington, Society for Research on Women in New Zealand Inc.

Social Development Council, 1980. *Families and Violence,* Wellington, Social Development Council.

Sorrenson, M., 1984. 'Maori and Pakeha', pp. 168-93 in W. Oliver (ed), *The Oxford History of New Zealand,* Wellington, Oxford University Press.

Spoonley, P., 1988. *Racism and Ethnicity,* Auckland, Oxford University Press.

Stace, M. 1983. *Rape Complaints and the Police,* Wellington, Institute of Criminology, Victoria University.

Steven, R., 1985. 'A Glorious Country for a Labouring Man', *Race, Gender, Class,* 1(1): 38-56.

Stivens, M. 1978. 'Women and their Kin', pp. 157-84 in P. Caplan and J. Bujra (eds), *Women United, Women Divided,* London, Tavistock.

Stone, J., Barrington, R., and Bevan, C. 1983. *The Victim Survey,* Wellington, Institute of Criminology, Victoria University.

Sullivan, T., and Thompson, K., 1984. *Sociology, Concepts, Issues and Applications,* New York, John Wiley and Sons.

Szaszy, M. 1973. 'Maori Women in Pakeha Society', Address to the United Women's Convention, Auckland, 15 September.

Tennant, M., 1986. ' "Brazen-faced Beggers of the Female Sex" Women and the Charitable Aid System, 1880-1920', pp. 35-54 in B. Brookes *et al.* (eds), *Women in History: Essays on European Women in New Zealand,* Wellington, Allen and Unwin/Port Nicholson Press.

Thompson, J., 1977. 'Marriage for Women? Not a Healthy Business!', Paper presented to the Women and the Health Conference, Wellington, February 14-18.

Titmuss, R., 1974. *Social Policy: An Introduction,* London, Allen and Unwin.

Tolson A., 1977. *The Limits of Masculinity,* New York, Harter and Row.

Toynbee, C., 1984. 'Gender, Work and Leisure in an Early Twentieth Century New Zealand Community', *New Zealand Cultural Studies Working Group Journal,* 8, Autumn, 20-8.

Treasury, 1987. *Government Management: Brief to the Incoming Government.* vol. 1, Government Printer, Wellington.

Von Dadelszen, J., 1987. *Sexual Abuse Study,* Research Series 7, Wellington, Research Section, Department of Social Welfare.

Waldegrave, C., and Coventry, R., 1987. *Poor New Zealand,* Wellington, Platform Publishing Co.

Walsh, D., 1964. 'New Zealand: A Recent Controversy', *Journal of the Polynesian Society,* 73(3): 340-2.

Wilkes, C., Davis, P., Tait, D., and Chrisp, P., 1984. *The New Zealand Class Structure,* Working Paper 1, Department of Sociology, Massey University, Palmerston North.

Winiata, M., 1967. *The Changing Role of the Leader in Maori Society: A Study in Social Change and Race Relations,* Auckland, Blackwood, and Janet Paul.

Wolf, M., 1985. *Revolution Postponed: Women in Contemporary China,* London, Methuen.

Index